BEGINNER GUITAR
Bootcamp

LEARN **100+ SONGS** IN 7 DAYS
Even if You've Never Played Before

VRENY VAN ELSLANDE

© ZOT Zin Publishing 2022

All rights reserved. No part of this publication may be reproduced, distributed, or transmitted in any form or by any means, including photocopying, recording, or other electronic or mechanical methods, without the prior written permission of the publisher.

1st edition

www.zotzinmusic.com

Ordering information: For details, contact the publisher at the web address above.

Editor: Dylan Garity

Layout design: Lazar Kackarovski
Cover design: Susan Beatriz Arévalo López

Cataloging-in-Publication Data

Van Elslande, Vreny.
Beginner guitar bootcamp: learn 100+ songs in 7 days, even if you've never played before / Vreny Van Elslande.
Santa Clarita, Calif. : ZOT Zin Publishing, 2022.
ix, 110 p. : ill.
ISBN 978-1-7353571-3-3
    1. Guitar — Instruction and study. 2. Guitar — Methods — Self-instruction.
    3. Guitar — Studies and exercises. I. Title.

I met Vreny in 2002, and started lessons with him more or less as a beginner. My time learning with Vreny gave me the clarity and organization I was after, and within only a couple years of starting lessons, I was touring internationally in bands and teaching guitar full-time on my own. Without a doubt, Vreny's teaching methods are the cornerstone of my musical education and my career as a teacher and touring musician. Few teachers in my life could transform the passion I had for learning so efficiently into real understanding and musical ability.

Michael Beach
Melbourne
michaelbeach.org

DO YOU ENJOY LEARNING FROM VIDEOS?
WOULD YOU LIKE TO PROGRESS EVEN FASTER?
ARE YOU READY TO LEARN WITH LESS EFFORT?

Sign up for the video lesson package that
teaches everything in this book at:

GuitarVoyage.com/BeginnerGuitarBootcamp

CONTENTS

Introduction 7
Trust Helps You Learn with Less Effort 9
Tools 12
How to Tune the Guitar 15
How to Hold the Guitar 18

DAY ONE

    Day 1: Four Chords & Twenty-Five Songs in One Hour 22
    Rhythm 25
    Strum Am Songs 34
    Day 1, Part 2: The E Chord 37
    Hurting Fingertips & Stretching 39
    Day 1, Part 3: The C Chord 41
    Still Day 1, Final Part: The F Chord 43

DAY TWO

    Day 2: Keep Practicing Yesterday's Chords 46
    Day 2: Dexterity Training 48
    Day 2: The Em Chord 50

DAY THREE

Day 3: The A Chord 53
Day 3: The D Chord 54
Day 3: The Dsus4 Chord. 55

DAY FOUR

Day 4: The G Chord 58
Day 4: The Dm Chord 60

DAY FIVE

Day 5: Two-Chord Songs 63

DAY SIX

Day 6: More Two-Chord Songs 67

DAY SEVEN

Day 7: Notable Easy Three-Chord Songs 76
Songs with More than Three Chords 78

How to Play Flat and Sharp Chords 79
Branching Out from There: Bar Chords 91
I, IV, V 95
Blues Songs 98
The Most Commonly Used Strum Rhythm 101
In Closing. 104
Acknowledgements 106
About The Author 108
Review 109
Contact Info 110

Introduction

CONGRATS on the start of your guitar journey! You're in for a fun rollercoaster ride.

Can you imagine that, even if you've never held a guitar before, you will already be able to play about a hundred songs within a week?

All it takes is:

1) Optimism: Feel the joy of having it already accomplished.

2) Confidence: Believe that you can do this. Yes, some things will be challenging. Embrace the suck. Find joy in being out of your comfort zone. Keep in mind that outside of your comfort zone is where the best learning takes place, and where you'll experience the most growth.

3) A willingness to learn and an openness to follow directions.

4) Persistence and patience.

5) Self-discipline and focus.

Self-discipline and focus are incredibly important here to achieve what the book title promises. The most crucial of all the traits mentioned in the list above is focus. You will probably be tempted to skip around the book. I totally understand; I would have a hard time with that myself when excitement and curiosity about the journey kick in. After all, it's difficult to resist the temptation to randomly thumb through the book, especially if you have an excited, curious mind that's anxious to find out what songs you'll be learning later and that's dying to find out ahead of time what the system is that will make it possible for you to learn so many in such a short time. However, all the time you spend thumbing through the book is time that could have been spent learning. One cannot learn that much that quickly while wasting time.

You will get the most out of this book if you delay that gratification of getting your curiosity satisfied in favor of diligently working through the book, page by page. Keep your focus on the journey. Keep your focus on the process. Stay in the present moment with each word you read and each exercise you perform. With the process being the main focus, work from beginning to end without skipping around unless specifically instructed to do so. Optimally utilize your focus, time, and energy by avoiding the temptation to randomly jump to new sections. The fact I've just said the same thing so many times in a row in so many different ways, only serves to emphasize how important I think this is for your progress and results.

All champions and top performers reach their world-class results because they kept their focus on the process. When you focus on the process, the destination takes care of itself. Trying to get a glimpse of the destination ahead of time is a distraction that will only slow down the results you could be getting if you focused on the process instead. This book you're holding is the map that outlines the trajectory of that process. Following this map is how you will get the extraordinary results that the book title promises.

Anyhow: there is a plan, a goal, a vision, and a strategy embedded in these pages. Whenever you're ready, take the driver's seat, and enjoy the ride!

Even though you might never have touched a guitar before, you're merely days away from impressing your friends, relatives, and loved ones with your playing. Be prepared to see their jaws drop in a couple of days when they hear you rock song after song on guitar.

There is nothing quite like that amazing feeling. It's priceless!

Trust Helps You Learn with Less Effort

I can imagine it must almost sound like a marketing gimmick: "Hey, when you buy MY product, you will be able to play one hundred songs in the next seven days, no prior experience required!" It's part of the reason why it took me a long time to overcome the reluctance to give the book this all too sales-y sounding subtitle. In today's world of empty promises, clickbait, and an overabundance of marketing slogans bombarding us everywhere all the time, it's become hard to assess what's for real and what is meaningless, time-wasting rubbish. Moreover, with today's deluge of information and opinions, it also has become exponentially more challenging to know who or what to trust. It sometimes seems like everyone and their grandma has suddenly become an authority or an expert on YouTube or on the internet.

The reality, though, is that most of these so-called experts all too often give very questionable advice. I've seen this with students who come to me for lessons after having learned from YouTube by themselves first. They often ask me, "Why do I still have wrist issues? I've been playing almost a year and my wrist still hurts a bit when I play guitar." Or, "Why is it still so hard to switch chords? Shouldn't this be easy by now? I've been playing six months already!"

I've seen it all: from students with terrible hand technique because that is how they saw it done in YouTube videos, to students whose strumming and coordination is all over the place because videos don't correct their timing, to students who have been learning from videos for months, yet have practically nothing to show for it in terms of progress and results, to students who are on a course to end up physically injured due to bad technique.

The only thing I have *not* seen yet in the past twenty-seven years of teaching, is someone who, learning from YouTube (or similar style resources), got really good in a very short amount of time, without also taking lessons with a teacher.

Because there is so much bad information out there eroding trust and credibility, and because trust is such an essential requirement for optimal learning, I owe it to you to first build up your trust a bit, so you can allow yourself to be freely open to all the information you're about to discover. Learning a hundred songs on guitar in seven days really is possible, even if you've never played before. It's a process. You will get the maximum results out of this resource, as long as you trust the process. Without trust, true deep learning is hampered. Trust instills confidence. Confidence that you can do this, confidence that the process works, confidence that you will achieve your goal of playing guitar. That confidence will help you learn faster and with less effort. Here are some quick, short, trust-building stories.

1) Music school in Belgium is a ten-year program. I finished the education in seven years. I progressed so well that my teacher and the school board decided to allow me to skip three years. To my knowledge, at that time, this was unheard of and had never happened before. I graduated in seven years, with high honors as a classical guitarist. I use the same processes and systems that made me progress that quickly to maximize the progress of my students.

2) At Berklee College of Music, I decided on a dual-major: Performance (guitar) and Music Production & Engineering. I finished the five-year dual major in a bit less than four years, getting both my degrees Summa Cum Laude.

3) My students all, without any exception, progress way faster than students of almost any other guitar teacher. Mind you, my main goal as a teacher is not for my students to "progress fast." My goal is for my students to have an unbelievable amount of fun learning guitar. It just so happens that one of the dominant factors that contributes the most to how much fun one has learning the instrument, is the cool feeling of achievement that kicks in when, in no time at all, you hear yourself play things on guitar that sound really amazing. Almost three decades of teaching guitar has given me hundreds of student success stories, but let me just keep it at two stories so we can get to actually playing soon.

First off, meet Olga. Olga walked into her first lesson with her beautiful white Strat, not knowing how to hold the guitar. But Olga was driven, and decided to meet with me twice a week. Exactly three weeks after she first started lessons with me as a complete beginner, Olga played AC/DCs "Highway to Hell" and Deep Purple's "Smoke On The Water" note-for-note, exactly as on the record.

You can check out the videos I shot from her lesson three weeks after she started out learning guitar, in the following blog:

https://www.zotzinguitarlessons.com/blog/this-is-why-everybody-wants-to-study-guitar-with-us/

Of course, Olga loves classic rock, but you can replace "Smoke On The Water" or "Highway to Hell' with any song or genre of your liking. Your musical styles and tastes might be different from hers, but your results are going to be equally outstanding.

4) One more story to illustrate why my students love their learning experience is that of Mike Beach. Mike showed up with his lefty acoustic guitar in his first lesson. He had just moved to Los Angeles from San Francisco only days before, after someone in San Francisco had recommended me as a teacher. As is the case with beginners, I guided Mike in how to hold a guitar in his first lesson, and he learned his first chords, rhythms, and songs. He came out of that lesson able to play his first songs along with the recordings. Fast-forward pretty much exactly three years from that day when Mike had his first guitar lesson with me. He moved to Melbourne and within two months became one of the busiest guitar teachers in the city, teaching students every week from his home studio. Mike literally went from beginner guitar student to professional musician earning his living with music only, in merely three years' time. He has a couple of albums out by now, and is currently preparing for his next (third or fourth, I lost count) international tour doing his own music.

These stories show that you're in the good hands of someone who really knows what he's doing, and that the likelihood you will be able to play a ton of songs by the end of this week is not a fad but a fact. These are some of the reasons why I ultimately decided that the book's overly ambitious subtitle was acceptable. Now that you might have enough reason to trust that you will actually get a ton out of this book, let's start the journey that lies ahead.

The first day of this journey will take about thirty minutes of reading and one hour of playing guitar. After that, there won't be all that much reading anymore. Starting on Day 2, you're going to be playing about an hour a day. That is all it takes to reach one hundred songs in seven day, and finish this book as a much better guitar player.

Tools

Here are some things you will need on this journey.

Capo

A capo is a clamp that, when placed on the neck of a stringed instrument, raises the pitch of the strings by a desired amount. Its name derives from the Italian *capotasto*, which translates to "head of the fretboard." In essence, it makes guitar necks shorter. When you clamp a capo on, say, the third fret, your guitar strings no longer start from the nut (also called "the zero fret"), but now start ringing from the third fret. As a result, a chord shape that, for example, was played on the first fret will now move up three frets to the fourth fret.

My favorite capos are made by the company Shubb. I like their smaller, compact size, which makes them look nice on the guitar neck. You can check out and get Shubb capos here: https://amzn.to/3mEU9Ck

Amazing Slow Downer

This is still the best song practice software out there. I use this software all the time, every day. As you can gather from the name, it allows you to slow down songs. It does so without changing the pitch of the song. Sometimes songs are just too fast to be able to keep up with. Some guitar solos are hard to figure out when the guitarist is speeding through a lot of notes. Learning these songs or solos becomes a lot easier when they're slowed down. Amazing Slow Downer does this exceptionally well, with very little sound degradation, even at extreme settings.

Conversely: Amazing Slow Downer also makes it possible to change the pitch of songs. That is a very useful feature for songs where the band didn't tune with a tuner before their recording session. Some examples of songs that sound out of tune when you try to play along with the song using a perfectly tuned guitar are "Highway To Hell" (ACDC), "Brake for Genius" (The Mercury Tree), and "It's The Singer Not The Song" (The Rolling Stones). One of my favorite guitarists, Greg Howe, has a song called "Come and Get it" on his album "Introspection," where the tuning falls between B and C. It's a sharp B and a flat C. The three main reasons why songs might sound out of tune in relation to an in-tune guitar are:

1) The guitar player in the band whose recording is flat or sharp tuned all six strings on his guitar in tune to one another without using a tuner, using a string on his guitar as reference that was not tuned to the standard 440Hz, and everybody else in the band then tuned to him. Result: everybody is in tune with one another in the band, so the song sounds right, but the band as a whole is tuned flat or sharp in relation to the 440Hz standard reference pitch.

2) The song was recorded on an analog tape machine that needed its tape speed calibrated, or something went wrong when transferring the song from the analog to the digital domain, which caused the playback pitch to be lower or higher than how the band performed the song during the recording session.

3) Some artists might deviate from tuning to the 440Hz tuning standard for sonic feel and mood, or creative reasons. That is what I think happened in the Greg Howe song. Greg Howe is too advanced a musician, and too meticulous, for this to have been something that happened by accident. In Greg's song "Come and Get It," the off tuning between the keys gives the song a very warm, moody, laid-back, unique sound and feel. The song would have had a very different feel and mood if it were played in the key of C on a guitar tuned to the standard 440Hz.

Then there are also guitar players who tune all strings down a half step. Stevie Ray Vaughan is one of those. Some guitarists prefer playing heavy-gauge strings because they feel those strings sound bigger and fuller. Those players usually then tune down a half step to relieve some of the extra tension and string tightness that you feel when playing thicker strings. Tuning all six strings down a half step relieves that tension and makes the guitar easier to play.

Amazing Slow Downer relieves you from the hassle of having to tune your whole guitar down to sound in tune with those songs. It's hard to get yourself to learn a song when you have to retune your whole guitar before you even get to start learning that song.

With Amazing Slow Downer, you can literally tune any song to your guitar in a matter of seconds. So much faster, so much easier, which will make you want to practice more.

You can find out more and buy the software here:

https://www.zotzinguitarlessons.com/amazing-slowdowner/

A Tuner

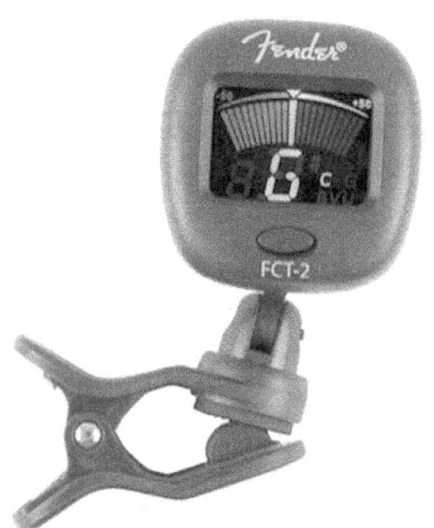

At this stage in your guitar-playing capabilities, you don't want to deal with the hassle of learning how to tune by ear. Get a clip-on tuner. They're very easy to use. You clip the tuner on your head stock. It reads the vibrations in the wood that are caused by the vibrating string and tells you on screen if the string is flat, sharp, or in tune. In the next chapter, I'll explain how to tune your guitar using a tuner. Enter the following URL in your browser to buy one of the better clip-on tuners.

https://amzn.to/3ynwetg

Speakers

Students often practice along with a song while listening to that song on their small built-in laptop speakers. While the technology has come a long way, and while it's astonishing how good and loud those little speakers sound, I find that they still tend to be a bit too quiet for students to hear the music well enough while playing along. In my teaching studio, I route the audio coming out of my iMac to my HiFi amp, which is connected to the big Pioneer speakers I have hanging off of my teaching studio wall.

Ninety-nine percent of the time, when I hear a student playing rhythmically uneven or out of sync with the music, simply turning up the volume fixes the timing issues. You will play with better timing and will feel the music better when you can play it loud enough. For that reason, I highly recommend you consider investing in speakers to connect to your computer. You can find pretty inexpensive computer speakers on Amazon for around twenty or thirty bucks. It's worth the investment — you will learn so much more easily when you can really hear the music that you're trying to learn or play along with.

How to Tune the Guitar

For starters, you want to memorize the open string names. These are the notes each string needs to be tuned to.

From bass (thickest) to treble (thinnest) string, the notes are

E A D G B E

You can speed up memorization with the following mnemonic:

"**E**very **A**pple **D**oes **G**ood **B**eing **E**aten."

Here's another good one:

"**E**at **A**ll **D**ay **G**et **B**ig **E**asy."

Make sure your clip-on tuner has working batteries. Usually, they are sold with the batteries included. Clip your tuner to your guitar's headstock. The headstock is the part of the guitar at the end of the neck, where all the strings are attached to their tuning mechanisms.

Press the ON button on your tuner. With many tuners, you need to press and hold for a second till the display switches on.

Now, when you hit a string, a letter will appear on the tuner's display. You can see an example of that in the above picture. The tuner in the picture shows that a G string was hit.

1) The string you hit is in tune when you see a green-colored light or (sometimes blueish) arrow positioned in the middle of the tuner's display.

2) When the red color lights up on the left of the display screen, that means the string is flat and needs to be tuned up.

3) Conversely, if the red color lights up on the right, that means that the string is sharp and needs to be tuned down.

Assuming that strings are wound correctly:

1) You tune a string UP in pitch when you turn the tuning mechanisms on your head stock counterclockwise.

2) You tune a string DOWN in pitch when you turn the tuning mechanism clockwise.

How can you tell when you're accidentally turning in the wrong direction? Easy: you can tell by following the progress on the tuner's display. For example, when you hit the thinnest string, and the display on your tuner says F, that string is tuned too high in pitch, because we need that string to be tuned to the note E. F comes after E in the alphabet, so F is higher because that string passed E in pitch. On the other hand, if you hit that E string, but your tuner says D, you'll need to tune up cause the string is tuned to a note that is below E in pitch. D comes before E in the alphabet. Walking up the alphabet is like walking up in pitch. However, if you turn in the wrong direction, suddenly you'll see C on your display, then B, etc., moving farther away from the letter E you were trying to tune to. That's a sign you'll need to change the direction in which you are turning the mechanism.

As you get closer to the sound and height of an E note, you will see the letter E appear on the display. But, depending on if you are tuning up or tuning down to get to that E, you will either first see red on the left or red on the right. When that happens, start turning more slowly. You're at the stage where your tuner says that the string is in the vicinity of sounding like an E note, but you need to fine-tune that string's intonation of that note. It's close to an E, but sounds a little bit off. As you keep fine-tuning with small, slow turns of the tuning mechanism, you gradually will see the red disappear till suddenly the tuner will light up green, or you will have a green line at the center of the display.

When that happens, that string is perfectly in tune and you can move on to the next string.

As is the case with anything new you learn, in the beginning you'll be a bit slow. Your first attempts at tuning your guitar may take five minutes or so. You'll quickly gain experience, learning how much and how fast you can turn the tuning mechanisms to get to the desired results. With time, tuning each string is only going to take you a couple of seconds per string.

Ideally, you always want to tune before you start playing, to ensure proper intonation. Most guitars tend to stay in tune well for many hours, sometimes even days. If you're playing a lot or strumming hard, though, a string might go out of tune every once in a while. You can tell when a string gets a bit out of tune, because chords start sounding wrong. When that happens, simply take a minute to check the tuning of every string and adjust where necessary.

How to Hold the Guitar

Where and How to Rest Your Guitar

You can rest your guitar on your right or left leg. I always highly recommend that students who play electric guitar do so with a strap. Because the body of an electric is so much thinner than the body of an acoustic guitar, you will be spending part of your hands and mental energy trying to "hold" the guitar or keep it in place. When you have the instrument strapped around your shoulder, the strap takes care of holding the guitar in place. This frees up your mind and your hands to use them for actual guitar playing. This is a non-issue with acoustic guitars, which have bodies that are broad enough for the guitar to have more stability when resting on your leg.

Ideally, for maximum, immediate progress, you'll want to sit the way a classical guitarist sits when playing music — with your guitar resting on the leg that is opposite your handedness. That is, your left leg when you're a righty (right leg for lefties). For this to work, you'll need to position your legs apart so the guitar can rest between. This is a far superior guitar positioning for learning. It centers your guitar in relation to your body, which brings the fretboard closer to you. This positioning also stabilizes your guitar more. It ensures that the guitar is resting between three anchor points: the right leg, the left leg, and the chest.

Most people learn to rest their guitar on the leg that is on the same side as their handedness (right-handed and resting the guitar on the right leg). That is one of *the* biggest reasons why they progress way more slowly. The guitar feels more wobbly tilting from left to right on the leg, since the only anchor point keeping the guitar in place is that leg. This makes it harder to finger chords, because the guitar feels like it's constantly moving. In addition, with the guitar now positioned more to the side of the body, instead of centered, the guitar neck tends to be pushed away (forward) from you, which makes it feel like you have to "reach" for the neck, instead of the neck being right there. That too slows down the development of one's ability to learn and shape new chords.

Physical Posture

Sit up straight, on the front of a chair, with both feet planted firmly flat on the ground. Don't cross your legs. Don't sit all the way back on your chair with your back touching the chair's back support. That way, you feel more in control, and your guitar is not restricted or pushed away from you by the chair's seating area.

Lay your strumming arm on the guitar body so only a small area right underneath your elbow touches the guitar body. Let the weight of that arm push down on the guitar body, so it tilts the guitar's gravity point, raising the headstock up closer to your face. Don't push, though — just let the weight do the work. This positions the guitar's neck where it becomes comfortable for the fretting hand to finger chords.

Fretting Hand Position

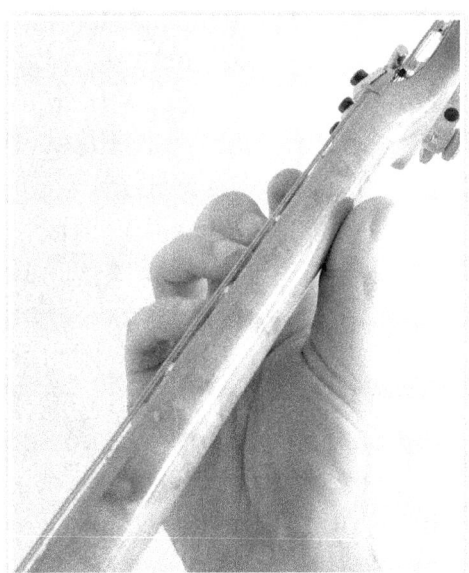

Now we've come to the most important part. This is where having bad technique can lead to injury.

Thumb

Keep your thumb behind the guitar neck. Don't grab over the neck: Keep it behind. Also, hold your thumb at about a 45-degree angle in relationship to the base of the wrist. In other words: you want to hold your thumb midway between forcing it inward and having it completely sideways. Notice in the picture how the thumb joint is completely straightened out. Many people make the mistake of bending the thumb joint at the joint under the nail, and then wonder why their forearm starts hurting after a while. In addition, notice the pincer grip, which is such a big deal in the development of infants. The picture shows how my thumb and index finger pretty much face one another, as if I'm picking up the guitar at the neck with a pincer grip. This is the most effective and efficient positioning of the fretting hand for guitar playing. Bring the thumb up higher over the neck, and you create tension in the tendons in the wrist. Bring the thumb more outward, and you lose grip and stability on the neck. Bring the thumb more inward, and you introduce tension into the muscle located between the thumb and the wrist. Bend your thumb at the joint, and not only do you lose stability on the neck, but you'll get an ache in your forearm after a while.

Resist the temptation to move your whole hand for certain chord changes. Many beginning and even intermediate guitar students push their wrist forward or move their thumb up the neck (toward the ceiling) when switching to a G or an A chord. It's not necessary to add in all this extraneous motion. You can finger these chord perfectly just by moving your fingers. Make sure to practice with minimal motion of the hand or thumb. Keep the thumb still, only moving the fingers from shape to shape. The less you physically move, the better and the more accurate your performance will be. Extraneous motion always results in poorer performance and lesser efficiency.

Wrist

Keep your wrist completely straight. No bend at the wrist: not inward nor outward. You want your arm to form a completely straight line from the elbow to the knuckles where the fingers meet the hand. The photo below shows perfect hand and wrist position.

All these guidelines fall under what we call guitar technique. You want to make sure that you perform every new chord, song, or chord switch with utmost focus on maintaining these technique standards at an optimal level. In almost three decades of teaching, none of my students have ever gotten injured. None of them have ever hit a plateau where they got stuck for long periods of time with no growth, as a result of having inadequate technique holding them back from reaching the next levels. The only way is forward. You'll see: Guitar is way more fun when played well.

DAY ONE

DAY 1

Four Chords & Twenty-Five Songs in One Hour

You're going to learn four chords in the next hour: Am, E, C, and F.

Notice how one of the chord names has a lowercase *m* in its name? Most songs primarily use two types of chords: major and minor chords. When there is no lowercase *m* in the chord name, then that is a major chord. When the *m* is present, then that chord is a minor chord. Major chords sound happy, upbeat, in your face, confident and bold. Minor chords sound sad, introverted, shy, and withdrawn.

Here's how you play the Am chord:

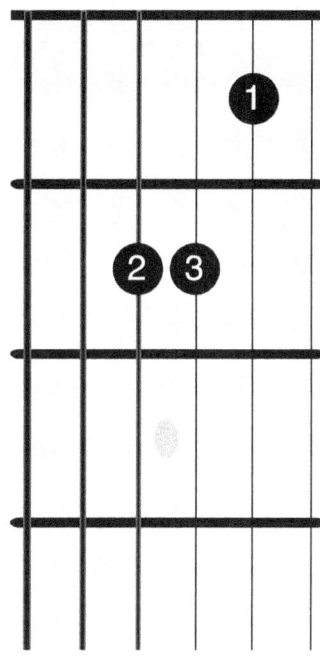

1) The vertical lines are the strings. You can tell by the line thickness that the string on the far left is the bass string, and the one on the right is the treble string.

2) The horizontal lines are the frets.

3) The dots show where to place the fingers.

4) The numbers in the dots show which fingers to use.

    i. 1 = index finger

    ii. 2 = middle finger

    iii. 3 = ring finger

    iv. 4 = pinky

For the fastest, most efficient result, you want to make it a habit to work through each chord diagram one finger at a time, always from left to right. Put your middle finger (2) on the D string (fourth string from the floor). Keep that finger there. Now add your ring finger (3) right underneath your middle finger on the string right below your middle finger, same fret. Keep those two fingers in place. Finally, add your index finger on the first fret of the second string.

Make sure that your thumb is behind the guitar neck, and that you are pressing down the strings with your fingers perfectly positioned on the fingertips. Don't press hard. You are merely trying to get the strings against the frets. Only press as hard as is necessary to accomplish just that. Now hit all six strings. That is what an Am chord sounds like. If you have a muted note here and there, spend a couple of seconds trying to improve your finger positions. Are you on the fingertips? Is your thumb behind the neck? Are you making sure your fingers are not slanted on the strings so you're not muting neighboring strings with the inside of your fingers? Are you pressing hard enough on the strings (but not too hard)?

You want to make sure you press enough for the strings to be against the frets, but not harder than that. You don't want to waste energy working your finger muscles harder. If after all that, the chord still sounds a bit muted, don't worry about it. Many of these issues will fix themselves as your hand muscles get stronger and your fingers more limber in the next couple of days. The way to get to that point in no time is to just play as much as you can.

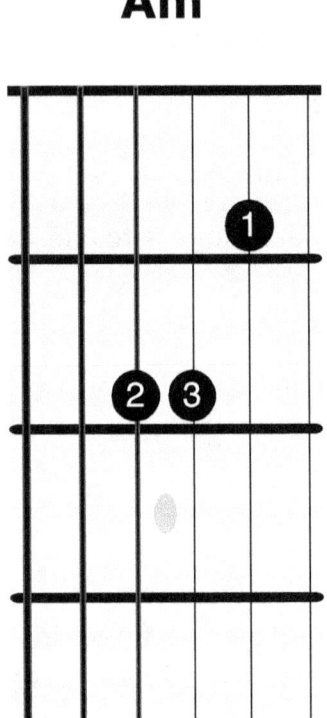

On the above chord diagram, the dots are nicely centered between the frets to make it easy to read the diagram. However, that is *not* how you want to position your fingers on the guitar. You want to position each fingertip right behind the fret for the best possible sound.

What does "right behind the fret" mean? It means that within that space between two frets, you want to slide your fingertips toward the guitar body till they are positioned, as much as possible, right next to the fret (as shown in this chord diagram). Pressing the string down in the middle between two frets, as shown in the above chord diagram, might cause strings to buzz against the fret.

Keep in mind, going forward, that for aesthetic and visual learning reasons, the dots will always be positioned nicely centered on the diagrams, but you always want your fingers positioned right behind the frets, never in the middle between two frets.

Extra tip to speed up chord memorization:

We'll be covering a lot of material in a relatively short amount of time. Here's some advice that will help you learn and memorize it all with less effort.

In these beginning stages, always look at your hand while playing, say the name of the chord you're fingering out loud, feel the sensation in your hand, and try to feel the shape and what it does to your hand and fingers.

That way, you are simultaneously activating more sensory learning systems in your brain: engaging the visual, the auditory, and the kinesthetic (feel, body, movement) information-processing centers all at the same time, which greatly enhances learning.

With all that out of the way, you're now really close to being able to play songs. The only thing we still need to discuss is how to strum.

Rhythm

Because the purpose of this book is not learning rhythms but learning how to play songs, we will only cover two rhythms. We will play all songs in this book with one of those two rhythms.

Rhythm is what you play when you strum the strings with your strumming arm. Strumming is what you do when you strike the guitar strings while you move your arm up and down. The point of rhythm is that you want to sync those arm motions with the beat (which is what we call the flow or the pulse) of the music. All songs have a beat, a certain pulse that drives that song. You can already tell where the beat is. The beat is where you are naturally inclined to bob your head for a song that you really like or that moves you. Right on the beat is where you move your head forward when bobbing along with the song. It's also where you count 1 2 3 4 | 1 2 3 4 | 1 2 3 4, etc.

While music has this driving pulse that we call a beat, every x number of beats sound like a repetitive cycle. That cycle is called a bar, or measure — the words are synonyms. Most music has four beats in a bar. This is best understood using children's songs as an example.

Twinkle, twinkle, little star,
How I wonder what you are!
Up above the world so high,
Like a diamond in the sky.
Twinkle, twinkle, little star,
How I wonder what you are!

Every lyric line in this song is one bar (four beats) long. This whole song-section is thus six bars long, since there are six vocal lines. The first word in every line falls right on the first beat, the last word in every line falls on beat number four.

Just to get a sense or deeper understanding of beats and bars, you should sing "Twinkle Twinkle Little Star" for a quick minute, tapping your desk or slapping your knee (or clapping your hands or bobbing your head) in an even pulse while singing.

In the first sentence:

- "Twin" in the first "twinkle" falls on beat 1
- "Twin" in the second "twinkle" falls on beat 2
- "Lit" in the word "little" falls on beat 3
- "Star" falls on beat 4

Immediately going into the next bar without interruptions between the beats,

- Beat 1 = "How"
- Beat 2 = "Won" in the word "wonder"
- Etc.

Each time your hand hits your desk or knee is a beat; every four times your hand comes down is a bar.

As it so happens in this children's song, two syllables fall on each of the first three beats in every bar, and there is only one syllable or word on beat 4. In other words: every two syllables fill up the space of one beat for beats 1, 2 and 3 in each of the six bars, and beat 4 only has one syllable.

The flow of the lyrics feels like (in terms of syllable count):

12 12 12 1
12 12 12 1
12 12 12 1
Etc.

When one sound (in this case a word or syllable) takes up the space of an entire beat, that is called a quarter-note rhythm. When two sounds (syllables) take up half a beat each, those durations are called eighth notes. Think of a bar as a pie. When you cut your pie into four even pieces, you have four quarters. When you cut those four quarters all in half, you get eight eighths. The sound durations taken up by the words are like pieces of a pie — in this case pieces of the bar.

When all this makes sense, then you're already half on your way to understanding how strumming works. As it turns out, when we play rhythm guitar, we always move our strumming arm twice per beat. Once down and once up. In other words: we move in eighths. Four beats in a bar times two arm motions per beat equals eight arm motions in a bar. There are of course more complicated rhythms that require moving the arm four times per beat or even three times, but none of these rhythms matter for what we're trying to accomplish here. In this book, we will only move twice per beat.

To reiterate: since there are four beats in a bar, and we will move our strum arm two times on every beat, that means that our arm is always going to move eight times in every bar.

- Down-up on beat 1
- Down-up on beat 2
- Down-up on beat 3
- Down-up on beat 4

Each individual arm motion takes up an eighth note, lasting for one eighth of the bar.

When you only hit in the down motions, and you miss the strings in all the up-motions, you are playing quarter notes. After all, when you hit the strings, and then you miss the strings on the next arm motion, the strings ring out for two arm motions. Right? That means that the sound is lasting for two eighths, since each arm motion equals one eighth of a bar. Two eighths is one quarter, the length/duration of one beat (since one beat is a fourth of a bar, as a bar is a collection of four beats).

Quarter Notes

This is the rhythm where you only hit the strings in the downstrokes and you miss the strings in all the ups. That is the easiest and hence the very best rhythm to start with when you've never strummed along with songs before.

It works like this:

Down *miss/up*   **down** *miss/up*   **down** *miss/up*   **down** *miss/up*

It looks like this btw in music notation.

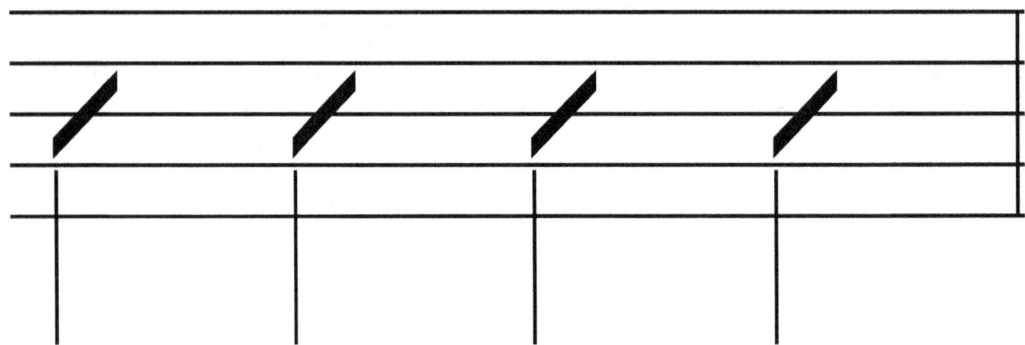

Try this out with your first song for today. Here's your first exercise.

Exodus (Bob Marley) → Am chord

Get Bob Marley's song "Exodus" from iTunes or pull it up on whatever streaming platform you use. Ideally you would want to hear the music through speakers, at a pretty loud volume. If you play electric guitar, you can also turn down your guitar completely in addition to boosting the volume on the song.

In case you can't figure out where the beats are in this song, which you need to know in order to know where to strum, know that the tempo of the song is around 132 bpm (beats per minute). Do the following to get a sense of how fast 132 bpm is:

- Google the word "metronome."
- In the metronome that shows up in the search result, there is a slider button that you can grab with your mouse.
- Drag that slider to the right till the number says 132.
- Make sure your computer volume is on and up.
- Then hit the play button on the metronome.

- The beeps/clicks you hear tell you how fast to move your arm.
- Every click signifies a beat. At this tempo, there are 132 beats in a minute.
- Your strum arm needs to move to the floor right on every click you hear.
- Your arm moves up in between the clicks.
- You want all your up and all your down motions to be perfectly the same in length.

Spend a minute moving your arm as described, along with this metronome set at 132. Make sure to hit the strings right on top of every click you hear. Don't hit the strings when you move up between the clicks.

Make sure to move big. Make big, strong arm motions.

This is really important. Make sure that your hand that's holding the pick moves all the way below and all the way above the six strings. If your strumming hand kind of keeps hanging in front of the strings, you are moving way too small. The stronger and the bigger you make the down and up arm swings, the easier and the sooner you will feel the rhythm. Your timing is also going to be much better when you move strongly. You will find it much easier to sync your arm motions and rhythmically lock in with the song when you move big.

Pretty cool, right?

When that minute is over, stop the metronome by clicking on its play button. Let's now play along with the song. You will be doing exactly what you just did, but along with the song instead of with the metronome.

Play "Exodus" right now and strum along. Do this for about two minutes. Notice how your hand lines up with the syllables in the lyrics. If not, adjust your speed or hand motions to sync up with the lyrics and rhythm section.

As an example: when you maintain an even hand motion, the hand moves down right on the syllable "ex", then up, then down again on "o," then up on "dus." When Bob is singing again a couple of bars later, all your down motions should fall together with the syllables — move-ment-of-Jah, with the up-motions falling in between those syllables, and right after the word "Jah" *on* the syllables "peo" and "ple." This should give you some sense of how listening to the syllable placement in vocals is usually a huge help in figuring out how fast to move your arm to be in sync with the music. I hope this helps.

This should start getting easier after about two to three minutes of practice. Keep in mind that you can always use Amazing Slow Downer to slow the song down a bit if you have a hard time keeping up with it or syncing your arm motions to the song. Slowing songs down can help a lot. If you feel you need a bit more practice in this before moving on to the next rhythm, put a capo right on top of the first fret, finger an Am chord right next to the capo, and play "Papa Was a Rolling Stone" with all downstrokes.

Besides the vocal syllable placement, also listen to the drums to help sync your arm. Every time you hear a kick and a snare, your arm should move down right on those parts of the drum kit. Drummers in rock and pop songs, for the most part, play like this: kick snare kick snare.

The kicks, the heavy, low-sounding hits which the drummer plays with the right foot pushing a pedal that hits the kick drum, are always played on beats 1 and 3 in each bar. The snare, which produces a snappy, sharp, bright hit, is played on beats 2 and 4. If you line up your arm motions to move down right on those drum hits, you are playing perfectly in sync with the whole song.

There's also the bass guitar. The heaviest, lowest, loudest notes in bass parts usually fall right on the beats. In other words, on downstrokes. When you listen for all this, you will find that it will get a lot easier to sync your arm motions with the song. This should give you enough pointers to help you tighten up your timing. "Papa Was a Rolling Stone" is a great song for training these listening and timing skills, as the mix of this song has the rhythm section (drum and bass) upfront and fairly loud in the mix.

Once you get the hang of hitting all downstrokes, quarter notes, in sync along with the song, you should move on to the next rhythm. Getting the hang of hitting on every downstroke in sync with the previous two songs, all in all, should not take more than six or so minutes.

As you can probably already tell by now after playing the above two songs for a couple of minutes each, you would not want to play a whole song just hitting quarter notes. That rhythm simply doesn't sound interesting enough. It probably didn't take too long before you started to feel bored when playing this rhythm. That's why you're ready for the next one.

Quarter Two Eights

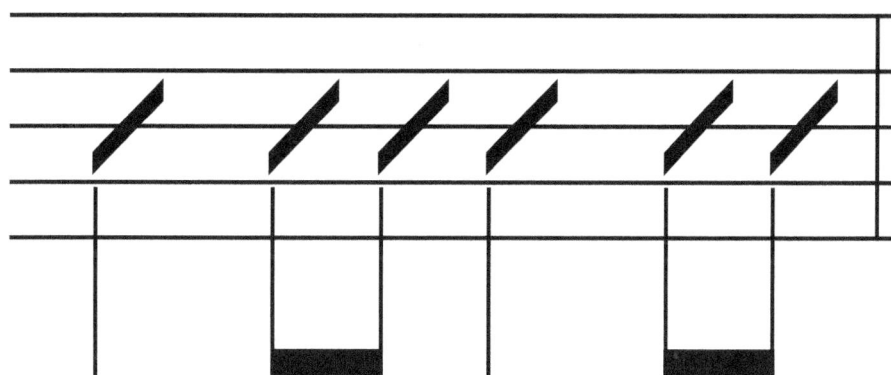

This is the rhythm we'll be playing for all the songs coming up in the book.

Notice the four beats. On the first beat, we play one sound. (That duration, as you already know, is called a quarter note. It looks the same as the notes in the previous rhythm). On the second beat, you now see two notes. This is how you notate two eighth notes. On the third beat, we play what we played on the first, and on the fourth beat, we play the same as on the second — two eighth notes.

Notice, in the above music notation, how the rhythm on the last two beats is simply a repetition of the rhythm on the first two beats.

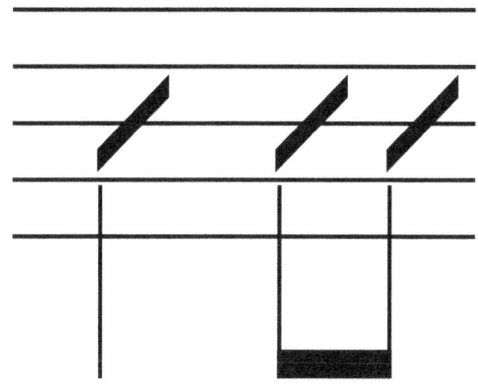

In other words, this is really a two-beat rhythm. If you can play just this, you can play the whole bar. You just need to play this two-beat rhythm pattern twice in a row to turn the rhythm into a four-beat bar.

Looking at the whole 4-beat bar: you can see that this rhythm consists of six hits. It has two more hits than the previous rhythm we played, as we are now also hitting in two of the four up motions.

Remember that the strumming arm always needs to move in a consistent, even (in length, speed, and duration) succession of eight "down-up" motions per bar (four downs, each one followed by an up). Keeping that in mind, here's how to play this new rhythm:

Down *miss(up)*   **down up**   **down** *miss(up)*   **down up**

Using different words, and keeping in mind that every word is one arm motion, I could also have written it like this:

Hit *miss*   **hit hit**   **hit** *miss*   **hit hit**

Or...

move *move*   **move** move   **move** *move*   **move** move (Understanding that we hit the strings on the black-colored moves and miss the strings on the grey-colored moves. The bold "moves" in this example are where the arm moves toward the floor)

Seeing the same rhythm explained, worded, or written three different ways might help your understanding of how this works.

Play this rhythm over and over again, nonstop, as a continuous piece of music, till you feel comfortable performing it.

An Important Note:

Rhythm playing is a physical more than a cerebral act. That is probably why, more often than not, I've seen it happening that a student's (over)thinking gets in the way of being able to figure out where to hit and where to miss. This is where it really pays off to get out of your way and out of your head.

Instead of thinking about it or trying to figure out how to play this rhythm using analytical skills or systems:

- Feel the arm motions — focus on the physical feel that comes with playing this rhythm. There is a feel and physical flow that comes with hitting once then missing once, then hitting twice in a row.

- Focus on recreating the specific sound of this rhythm: taaa tata taaa tata | taaa tata taaa tata| etc.

- Resist the tendency to turn this into a counting or a math exercise. It's a long sound followed by two shorter sounds, over and again. Let the sound guide your arm.

Spend no more than three minutes on this. That is really all you need. Make sure that you focus really hard on not stopping the strumming arm. You hit then you miss, then you hit on the next two arm motions, then without stopping the arm swings, you immediately do that again, and again, and again, creating a repetitive, even rhythmic flow.

When you've practiced that for a few minutes, move on to the next chapter. This is the rhythm we'll use to strum all the upcoming songs.

Strum Am Songs

Great news: at this point, you've worked through most of the reading in this book. There won't be that much text or explanation going forward. You now have the entire foundation and all the basics down to get you through the next hundred songs and the rest of the book. Things will start moving fast now.

Keep in mind that when you have a hard time playing that new rhythm along with the song, slowing the song down 10 to 30 percent (or more if necessary), will make it a lot easier to play. I strongly encourage you to get Amazing Slow Downer and use it. Only slow a song down, though, if it is really way too fast. If you *can* pull off the song at full speed, even when doing so is difficult, you should avoid slowing it down. Push through the challenges, rather than bypassing them. That is how you get champion results. You should only use Amazing Slow Downer if a song is so fast that your rhythm playing along with the song is 70 to 90 percent wrong, out of sync or all over the place. If you can pull off a song at about 60 percent accuracy, or in other words with about 40 percent mistakes or sync issues, you should keep plowing forward at the song's full speed. Optimum progress lies in the process of trying to fix things on the go while the song keeps moving forward. Keep in mind that, with each successive song, your timing and strum coordination is going to keep getting better. You don't need to get it all perfect in the first couple of songs. After all, we're using that same rhythm for *all* the upcoming songs. It's going to keep getting a lot of practice.

Play the first two minutes of the next two songs. Don't play the full song. If you can play about two minutes of the song, you can play the whole song. All the rest is just repetition.

Again, crank the music so it is loud through your speakers, and turn your guitar volume down if you're playing an electric. Move big with your strumming arm. Put all your focus on listening to the beat and feeling the beat. Notice how your arm motions all coincide and line up with syllables in the vocals. Notice how your arm motions all fall on drum hits and on heavy bass notes in the bass player's part. This is the case in every song. If your arm motions don't line up, immediately take action to correct your placement so you get back in sync with the song. You can also just stop playing, then drop in again. Don't stop the song. Instead, try to keep up and try to get back on when you get lost. Constantly course correct your sync and timing, till staying in sync becomes second nature.

Have fun with these two songs. Again: only play two minutes each.

1. **Exodus** (Bob Marley) → Am
2. **Madeleine-Mary** (Bonnie Prince Billy) → Am

How did that go? If you were a bit all over the place, no worries — it's going to get a bit easier with each new song you tackle.

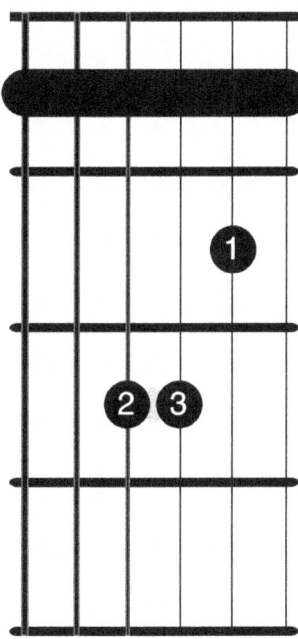

Bbm

The next couple of songs are in the key of Bbm (B-flat minor). That is why you needed to get a capo. Bbm is what you get when you play an Am chord shape up a fret, with a capo on the first fret.

You can tell in this chord diagram what that looks like. The thick line shows you where to clip your capo on the neck. Actually, in line with the comments made earlier about finger placement needing to be right behind the frets, you would want your capo to be right behind the first fret for best results. In terms of capo placement, it's even acceptable to place a capo on top of the fret. Some capos exert so much tensile strength that they might push strings sharp, even when nicely placed right behind the fret. Putting the capo right on top of the fret wire prevents that from happening.

You know the drill. For the next two songs in the list, only play the first two minutes, then move on to the next song.

3. **Papa Was a Rolling Stone** (The Temptations) → Bbm (Am chord moved up a fret with a capo on the first fret). You may have already played this song earlier; now do it with the down down up down down up rhythm.

4. **The Enchanted Gypsy** (Donovan) → Bbm
   This song is a waltz. Strum ||: down (miss) down up down (miss) :||

That is enough Am chord practice. **Move on to the next chapter to learn the E chord.**

Come back and play the remainder of the Am chord songs below on this page tomorrow (or whenever you want to).

The next five songs are in Bm (Am chord played with capo on the second fret). Bm is Bbm moved one fret up from the first to the second fret. In other words: take your capo off the first fret, and now clip it on the second before playing these following songs.

5. **Crosseyed & Painless** (Talking Heads) → Bm
6. **Get the Party Started** (Pink) → Bm
7. **The Hustle** (Bars of Gold) → Bm
8. **Nevermind** (Leonard Cohen) → Bm

For the following song, in Cm, move the Am shape up three frets, which is done by playing with a capo on the third fret.

9. **Get Up Stand Up** (Bob Marley) → Cm (capo on 3)

DAY 1

Part 2: The E Chord

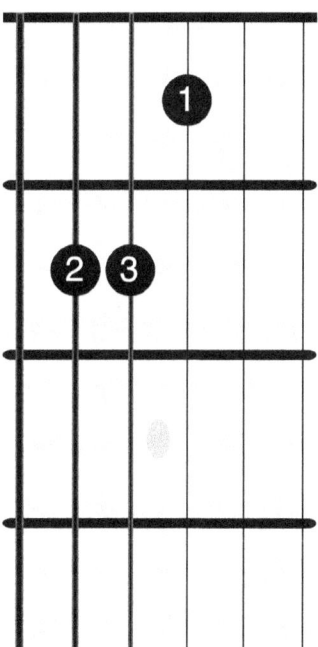

Are you seeing yet why my students all progress so quickly? Almost every teacher starts their beginner guitar students on songs that have way too many chords, or teach the chords following an order where the student has to move too many fingers all at once, or where the chord shapes are visually too different from one another, which makes it harder to remember the shapes.

The most logical next chord to learn after Am is the E chord. It's exactly the same shape, just up a string.

Move your first three fingers up one string toward the ceiling, and you're playing an E chord. Not too bad, right? Now, don't let the fact that it's the same shape fool you into thinking Am and E must be related somehow or have a lot in common. They're two completely different chords. Guitar is funny that way. Piano is much more straightforward and much easier to make sense of. The logic behind why, on a guitar, a same shape can be two entirely different chords has to do with how the strings on a guitar are tuned in relation to one another. That knowledge is not important enough, and too complicated for now, to get into. Back to playing.

Using everything you've learned so far, play the first two minutes in the next three or four songs. Play two minutes of "Seeds," then two minutes of "Spoonful," two minutes of "Who Do You Love," and, if you so desire before moving on to the next chord, also two minutes of "Walking in Your Footsteps."

That should take about eight minutes. Override the temptation to play more of the E songs below. Practice the remaining ones tomorrow, or whenever you feel like.

10. **Seeds** (Bruce Springsteen) → E

11. **Spoonful** (Cream) → E

12. **Who Do You Love** (George Thorogood version) → E (You might have to slow this song down a bit).

13. **Walking in Your Footsteps** (The Police) → E

14. **Mondo in Mi 7a** (Adriano Celentano) → E

Play the remaining songs tomorrow or later. Move on to the C chord after first learning about stretching on the next page.

15. **Moanin' At Midnight** (Howlin Wolf) → E

16. **Pric** (Super Furry Animals) → E

17. **The Story of One Chord** (Mojo Nixon and Skid Roper) → E

18. **Whole Lotta Love** (Led Zeppelin) → E

19. **Keep on Chooglin'** (Creedence Clearwater Revival) → E

Before moving on to the next chapter, play an Am chord again. Then play an E chord again.

Repetition is the mother of retention.

Before moving on to the C chord, let's give your brain *and* your fingers a quick break, with a short read.

Hurting Fingertips & Stretching

Fingertip Soreness

You've been playing for about twenty minutes now, and your fingertips might be getting sore. You can either choose to stop to give your fingers some rest, or you can push through the discomfort. I would recommend you keep going for thirty to forty more minutes, till we've finished all of today's chords. We're pretty much halfway now.

If you keep pushing forward through the fingertip soreness now, your fingertips will get much stronger in a much shorter amount of time. It's only a matter of days then before they are no longer going to get sore. If you take things easier now, it might take up to two or three weeks before your fingertips stop getting sore.

To alleviate some of the soreness, take regular quick, short breaks to massage the tips of the sore fretting hand fingers with the thumb of your picking hand. This stimulates blood flow to the fingertips, which after a couple of seconds diminishes the pain. You can of course also break up your practice, take a break, and come back later in the day to continue on to the C chord.

The Two Stretches

Also, take a moment to stretch the tendons and muscles in your fretting arm. There is no need to do this with the strumming arm. Rather than me giving a lengthy description here, watch the following one-minute video to learn how to perform the two stretches.

https://youtu.be/WgZ9WDBE5Wk

You should do these stretches right now. It will only take one minute, but it will pay off a thousandfold in much faster progress. After doing these stretches, you might find that your fretting hand is suddenly performing much better, as if your hand suddenly gained strength in addition to flexibility. You might find that everything has suddenly gotten a lot easier on guitar after stretching, as if you've just become a much better player.

It's normal to experience that sensation after those stretches. The reason is that stretching not only relaxes and stretches your tendons and muscles, it also builds actual strength. It lengthens the muscle tissue and increases flexibility, which allows the muscle to move with greater range of motion, giving that muscle more strength as a result. This is the reason why all physical therapists and top personal fitness trainers recommend stretching regularly as part of fitness and strength training. Do those two stretches about every fifteen or so minutes. Now that your hand and brain have gotten some quick rest, let's get back to playing guitar.

DAY 1

Part 3: The C Chord

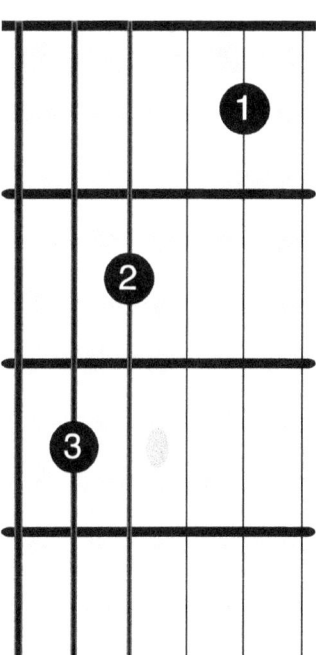

Can you tell why we're doing the C chord next?

Not sure if you see it, but this is almost like the Am chord you already learned, with only one finger different.

Do you still remember the Am chord? That's right: it's what you get when you finger an E chord shape, and then move all three fingers down one string.

Play the Am chord. Now, in that Am chord, lift up your ring finger from the third string, and place that finger, without moving the other fingers, on the third fret of the second thickest string (this is the A string, which is the fifth string counting from the floor up). Bingo: a C chord. Take a minute to look at your fingers and compare what you see on the fretboard to the picture on the left.

As always, play nicely on the fingertips, keeping your thumb behind the guitar neck. Press hard enough for the strings to land on the frets, but not harder than is necessary.

Play the first two minutes of the following three songs in the list.

20. **Chain of Fools** (Aretha Franklin) → C

21. **Coconut** (Harry Nilsson) → C

22. **Ever So Lonely** (Monsoon) → C

Play the following two songs tomorrow. For now, move on to the F chord on the next page.

23. **Tomorrow Never Knows** (The Beatles) → C

24. **Within You Without You** (The Beatles) → C# (C chord moved up a fret, with a capo clipped on the first fret)

STILL DAY 1

Final Part: The F Chord

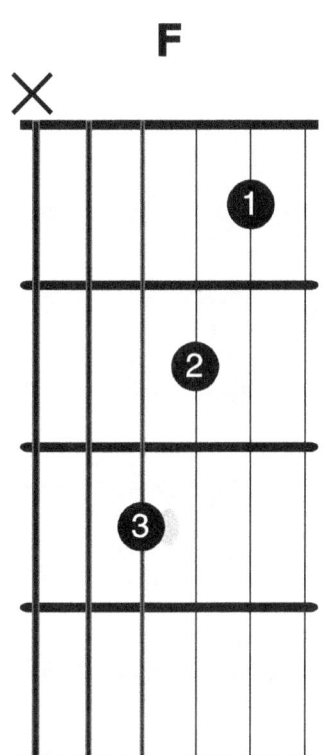

This is the last chord for today. If you're still with me, you're doing fantastic.

Notice how easy it is to learn the F chord when you already know C. You get an F chord when you move your middle and ring finger in a C chord one string down toward the floor.

In an F chord, the finger tips form a perfect diagonal line.

The X is new. X's placed above certain strings in chord diagrams show which strings not to hit.

In the previous chords you've learned, you can hit all six strings. While you can also do so in this F chord, the chord does sound better if you avoid hitting the bass E string. But don't worry about that for now.

I don't want you to start messing with your strumming so early in the process just so you can avoid hitting that string. Just keep in mind, for future reference, that that is what an X means in a chord diagram, but keep strumming exactly as you were already doing. If it's possible or if it's doable to avoid hitting your low E string or to hit that bass string less hard, feel free to do so. If not, don't spend time on trying to do this. It will slow you down and it's not important enough for now. Your F will sound just fine, even if there is a low E ringing underneath it. You might wonder why there's an X on only one of the two E strings. The reason why I didn't place an X above the treble E string is that the treble E note adds character and richness to the F chord, while the low bass E note obscures and muddies up the sound of the F chord with its low-frequency rumble underneath.

Since this is the last chord for today, spend however long you want to playing along with the following F chord songs after you've played the first three for two minutes each.

25. **The Beat Goes On** (Sonny & Cher) → F
26. **John Henry** (Buster Brown) → F
27. **The Story of Bo Diddley** (The Animals) → F
28. **Send Me Your Pillow** (John Lee Hooker) → F
29. **Which-A-Way Do Red River Run** (Mance Lipscomb) → F
30. **Ding Dang** (The Beach Boys) → F
31. **Peter Gunn** (Henry Mancini) → F
32. **See My Jumper Hanging on the Line** (R. L. Burnside) → F

All this should have taken about an hour. Including all the reading, you should have reached this point in about an hour and a half to an hour and forty minutes.

Definitely do the two stretches again now.

If you still have the energy or time, and only if, feel free to play more of the Am, E, C, and F songs.

Obviously, the more you play, the sooner you will get very good. But it can also be good to just rest your hand for the rest of the day. Regularly massage your fingertips.

If you can, every couple of hours or so, just pick up your guitar for a quick minute and finger the four chord shapes you learned in the past hour. For each shape you play, look at your fingers and name the chord name out loud, so you can make the link between how the shape looks and feels and its name. You'd be surprised how quickly you'll memorize the chord shapes and their names as a result of having those couple of quick one- or two-minute mini-rehearsals spread out throughout the day.

If you've reached this point, I've got to tell you: You did an absolutely fantastic job.

I'm not prone to throwing out compliments just for the sake of doing so. I only give them when I mean them. If you've managed to reach this point, in just one day, and you still pretty much retain the chords, then that is a major accomplishment.

DAY TWO

DAY 2

Keep Practicing Yesterday's Chords

You can now play thirty-five songs, and that's after only one lesson. I understand that you might feel that you can't play those songs very well yet, but that will come in the next couple of days. We'll only cover one new chord today, in the next chapter, and as you will see, it's a very easy chord.

Not having tons of new chords to deal with today opens up your focus to keep training that rhythm. Strumming should start getting a lot easier today. Today's practice schedule also leaves extra time to deeply train all the basics we covered yesterday. Here's a quick recap of things you want to keep checking with awareness:

1) Are you sitting right?
2) Are you holding your guitar on the leg opposing your handedness?
3) Are you keeping your thumb behind the neck and your wrist straight?
4) Are your fingers nicely on the fingertips, and positioned right behind the frets?
5) Are you making sure not to press too hard on the strings?

6) Are you playing the music loudly enough, and actively listening for aural cues in the song (snares, kicks, bass notes, syllables, etc.) to navigate your sync and line up your timing?

7) Are you moving big?

8) Are you remembering the four chord shapes?

9) Are you stretching regularly?

Have fun with the four chords you learned yesterday.

Starting right now:

1) Play Am chord songs for 10min (preferably songs you haven't played yet, the ones that you skipped yesterday).

2) Play E chord songs for 10min.

3) Play C chord songs for 10min.

4) Play F chord songs for 10min.

Done with all that? Great! We still have about twenty minutes.

Now, let's get your dexterity to the next level in the following chapter.

DAY 2

Dexterity Training

Dexterity means finger independence. So far, we've only played one-chord songs. It's when you start switching chords that you train your brain and fingers for dexterity.

For two minutes:

||: Am | C :|| (Strum one bar Am followed by one bar C, repeating both bars nonstop for two minutes. ||:   :|| is how you notate repeat signs in music notation. You repeat what's in between ||: and :||)

This is a good way to start your first steps into dexterity training, since only one finger needs to move (the ring finger).

Start out with the quarter notes rhythm, downstrokes only, switching chords every four hits.

Don't stop strumming, even if the fretting hand is having a hard time with the switch. Consistently keep switching the chord every four hits.

As soon as this gets easier, which typically happens in less than a minute, switch to the "down (miss) down up down (miss) down up" rhythm. You might want to slow down or play slowly enough so that you can play that rhythm and switch the chords at the same time, without dropping a beat.

For the next two minutes:

||: C | F :||

Now two fingers move from chord to chord. Use exactly the same practice approach as outlined above.

For the next two minutes:

||: Am | F :||

The same two fingers move from chord to chord, just in different ways than from C to F.

For the next two minutes:

||: Am | E :||

This is the most challenging move so far: all fingers move up and down the strings. Again, start with the downstrokes rhythm only, till you can switch without missing a beat. Then switch to the other rhythm.

If you still feel like it, for the next two minutes, practice:

||: F | E :||

And for two minutes:

||: C | E :||

This concludes every possible motion between all the chords you learned yesterday.

With eight more minutes to spare, let's move on to the next chapter, which is the last thing to do today.

DAY 2

The Em Chord

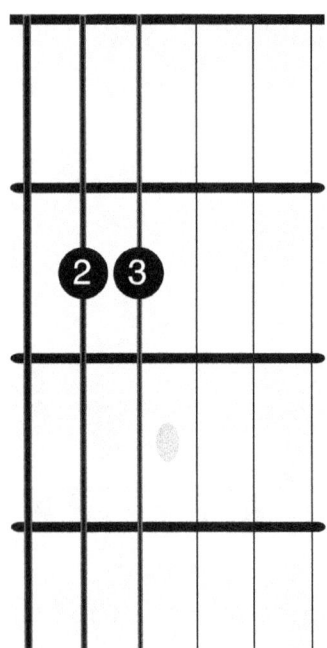

Em

As you can tell, this is an E chord minus the index finger.

I'm sure fingering this shape is a piece of cake for you now. In addition, by now, you probably don't need all that much guidance anymore to figure out the chord diagrams.

Here's a memory trick to avoid confusing E (major) and Em. We need **more** fingers to play E because it is a **major** chord. Em (minor) is smaller, a smaller shape, less fingers. More for major, less for minor.

You know the drill. We'll just keep doing what we did in the first day. Play a couple of minutes of the following songs.

Since we've finished all of today's tasks, you can play as many of the following songs as you want, you can play more C, Am, F, or E songs however you feel like, or you can rest your hand.

33. **Thank You** (Falettinme Be Mice Elf Agin) (Sly and the Family Stone) → Em

34. **Relax** (Frankie Goes to Hollywood) → Em
35. **Know** (Nick Drake) → Em
36. **Watussi** (Harmonia) → Em
37. **Pablo Picasso** (Modern Lovers) → Em
38. **Smokestack Lightnin'** (Howlin' Wolf) → Em
39. **I Asked for Water** (Howlin' Wolf) → Em
40. **I'm Bad Like Jesse James** (Howlin' Wolf) → Em
41. **Hallo Gallo** (Neu!) → Em (You might have to slow this one down)
42. **Powertruth** (35007) → Em
43. **Bodak Yellow** (Money Moves) (Cardi B) → Em
44. **What Are Their Names** (David Crosby) → Em
45. **Radar Eyes** (Godz) → Em
46. **Locker** (35007) → Em
47. **Paradise** (Sade) → Fm (Em chord moved up one fret with a capo on the first fret)
48. **Don't Worry (If There's a Hell Below, We're All Going to Go)** (Curtis Mayfield) → F#m (Em chord moved up two frets with a capo on the second fret)
49. **Political World** (Bob Dylan) → F#m
50. **Losing Face** (Snow Angel) → F#m

DAY THREE

DAY 3

The A Chord

A

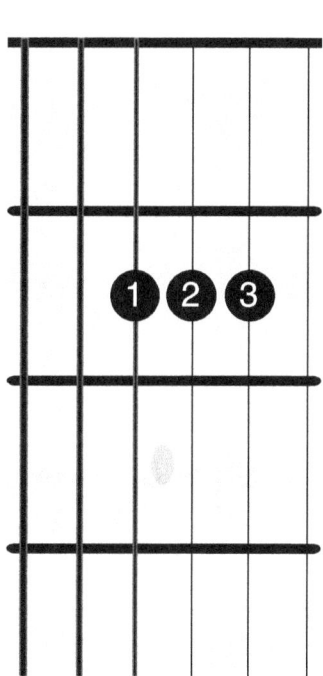

Before tackling this new A chord, spend a quick minute to first refresh your mind on how to play the Am, E, C, F, and Em chords.

When you've played all those shapes once more, it's time to have a look at the A chord. Notice how an A chord looks like an Em chord moved down a string, with a finger added underneath. Three adjacent fingers, pressing down three adjacent strings, all on the same fret.

Let's play some of the following songs in the key of A for about ten minutes.

51. **Electric Avenue** (Eddie Grant) → A
52. **Drifter's Escape** (Bob Dylan) → A
53. **There Is a Mountain** (Donovan) → A
54. **Helen Wheels** (Paul McCartney) → A
55. **Joy** (Lucinda Williams) → A

DAY 3

The D Chord

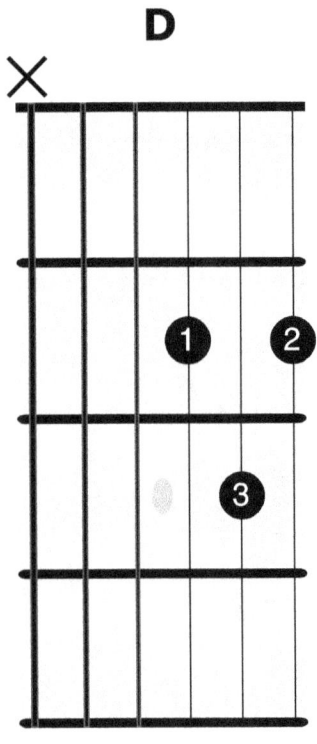

Notice how a D chord is a bit like an A chord moved down a string, with the note in the middle moved one fret forward.

Have fun playing some of the following songs for about ten minutes (set your timer). Have fun!

56. **Ohm** (Yo La Tengo) → D

57. **Church of Anthrax** (John Cale & Terry Riley) → D

58. **Loser** (Beck) → D

59. **Jump Into Fire** (Harry Nilsson) → D

60. **National Anthem** (Radiohead) → D

61. **One Chord Song** (Stoney LaRue) → D

DAY 3

The Dsus4 Chord

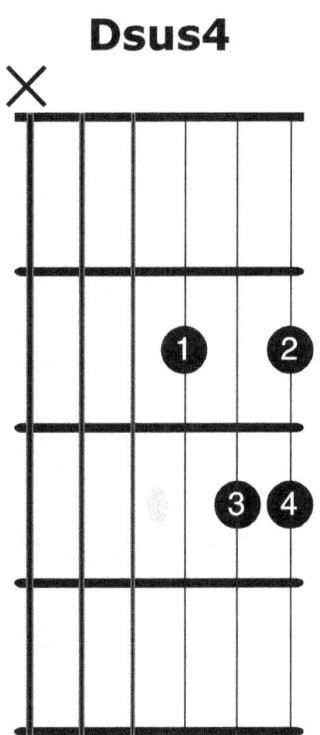

Dsus4

As you can see, a Dsus4 chord is the same as a D chord, but with the pinky added underneath the ring finger. The sus in the chord name, is an abbreviation for "suspended." Don't worry about the theory behind the name sus4. For now just memorize this shape and its chord name.

Have fun going back and forth between D and Dsus4. This is great training for the pinky, which is the weakest finger on the hand.

The sus chord is usually followed by its non-sus version in songs. Meaning: Dsus4 is usually followed by D, Esus4 by E, and so on.

This is a sound you hear a lot in classic rock. You can hear a ton of sus4 chord sounds in the intro to "Brown Sugar" (The Rolling Stones) or the guitar part in Tom Petty's "Free Fallin'", which we'll play in the next couple of days.

For the next three minutes:

1) ‖: A | D :‖ Practice going back and forth between A and D. First play downstrokes only, switching the chord every four hits. When switching gets easier, speed up a bit. Keep speeding up to keep challenging yourself. When you can switch at a pretty good tempo, practice switching with the "down down up" rhythm pattern, starting at a much slower tempo again. Do this for about three minutes.

2) For the remainder of the time, up to an hour total, go over all previously learned chords and songs again. The more regularly you keep repeating previously learned shapes, the sooner all chords will stick to memory.

DAY FOUR

DAY 4

The G Chord

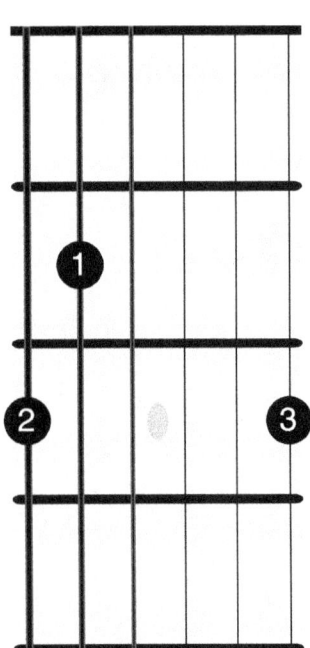

This is the biggest of all the chord shapes you will learn in this book. It spans all six strings, with a finger on the thinnest and a finger on the thickest string.

Interestingly enough, while you would think that the stretch this requires would make this a chord everyone struggles with in the beginning, most beginning guitar students tend to name G as their favorite chord. I'm not quite sure if this is because of its sound, but I suspect beginning students feel that way about G because it's easier to ring out all the notes in this chord, since it contains three consecutive open strings in the middle of the chord shape.

Whatever the reason might be, whenever I ask beginning guitar students what their favorite chord is, more often than not they answer G.

You know the drill. Here are the songs. Spend about fifteen minutes playing those G chord songs. Start with the first three songs in the list, about two minutes each. You can then freely pick and choose from the rest of the list.

62. **Low Rider** (War) → G
63. **Dance to the Music** (Sly and the Family Stone) → G
64. **Bad to the Bone** (George Thorogood) → G
65. **One Chord Song** (Keith Urban) → G
66. **It's a Rainy Day Sunshine Girl** (Faust) → G
67. **My Jack Don't Drink Water No More** (Shortstuff Macon) → G
68. **U.S. 41** (Tom Petty) → G
69. **Everyday People** (Sly and The Family Stone) → G
70. **Bo Diddley** (Bo Diddley) → G
71. **Spike Driver Blues** (Mississippi John Hurt) → G#/Ab (G chord moved up a fret with a capo on 1)
72. **Who Do You Love** (Bo Diddley version) → G#/Ab
73. **Catfish Blues** (Robert Petway) → G#/Ab
74. **Shotgun** (Jr. Walker) → G#/Ab
75. **Magic Bus** (The Who) → G#/Ab
76. **Rubberband Girl** (Kate Bush) → G#/Ab
77. **Boring Girls** (Pissed Jeans) → G#/Ab

DAY 4

The Dm Chord

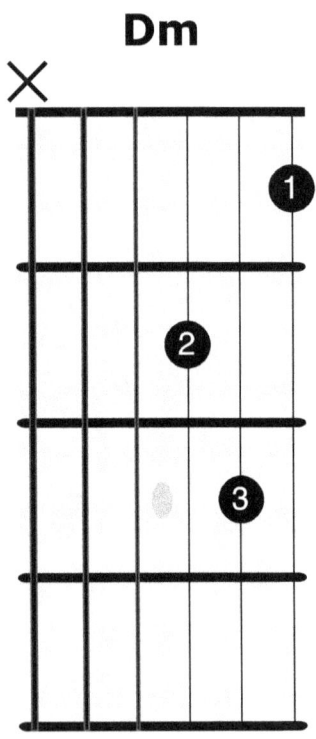

Guess what? Amazingly, this is actually your very last chord to learn in this book. There won't be any more chord shapes to learn after this. Notice how Dm is like a D chord with the note on the thinnest string moved one fret down, from second to first fret.

I kept this chord for last because this tends to be the one chord students seem to have the most trouble fingering.

Have fun playing the following songs. Spend about ten to fifteen minutes playing any of the following Dm songs.

78. **Run Through the Jungle** (CCR) → Dm

79. **Daydreamer** (Menswear) → Dm

80. **Showbizz Kids** (Steely Dan) → Dm

81. **Careful With That Axe, Eugene** (Pink Floyd) → Dm

82. **Machine Gun** (Jimi Hendrix, Band of Gypsys album version) → Dm

83. **Voyage Automatique** (35007) → Dm

Unbelievably, you can now play eighty-five songs at this point, and that's with three more days to go. This comes to show that, even if you kept a more relaxed pace than I outlined in this book so far, you still very well might be on track to learn a hundred songs in a week or less. Keep in mind that your performance of those songs is going to keep improving a lot in the next three days.

For the next thirty or so minutes:

1) Play one or two G chord songs, two minutes each.

2) Then play two Dm chord songs, two minutes each.

3) For memory and performance purposes and training, play one song for any of the previous chords you learned in past days, two minutes each. That is a fourteen-minute drill.

4) For the next ten minutes, take any random combination of two chords, and practice yesterday's dexterity drill with those two chords (two minutes each). For example:

   a. ||: D | Em :||

   b. ||: A | Em :||

   c. ||: D | F :||

   d. ||: A | C :||

   e. ||: C | Em :||

   f. Etc.

DAY FIVE

DAY 5

Two-Chord Songs

Hooray! You are done with all the one-chord songs. The dexterity drills you've been doing in past days will really pay off now. This is the next level: strumming songs that have two (and later more) chords. You will be switching chords now.

Play as many of those following songs as you feel like. To get the most amount of training in the shortest amount of time with the most possible chord combinations, maybe only play one or two songs for each of the following two-chord progressions, and then move on to a song that combines two other chords. Rather than randomly picking and choosing songs, you want to work your way down the following list, going in order from one two-chord combination to the next, playing two songs for each. The songs are listed in order of chord switching difficulty. First C to Am songs, where only one finger needs to move, then C to F songs, where two fingers move, then C to Em songs, where two other fingers move, etc., all the way to three fingers moving from chord to chord.

84. **Sexy Mary Brown** (Ferre Grignard) → ||: C | Am :||

85. **Only Want You** (Eagles of Death Metal) → ||: Am | C :||

86. **Hey Lover** (Blake Mills) → ||: C | F :||

87. **Feeling Alright** (Joe Cocker) → ||: C | F :||

88. **Heroin** (The Velvet Underground) → ||: C | F :|| (with capo on 1st fret)

    At 00:30 seconds, play at a faster tempo.

89. **Hold On** (Alabama Shakes) → ||: C | C F :||

90. **Reggae Got Soul** (Toots & the Maytals) → ||: C | C | F | C :||

91. **LDN** (Lily Allen) → ||: F C :||

92. **I'll Take You There** (The Staple Singers)

    Intro: ||: C | F C :||

    Verse: ||: C | F :||

93. **Something in the Way** (Nirvana) → ||: Em | C :||

94. **Closer** (Ne-Yo) → ||: C | C | Em | Em :||

95. **Only Want You** (Eagles of Death Metal) → ||: A | C :|| Same song as #87 above. You can play this song with either A or Am.

96. **A Horse With No Name** (America) → ||: Em | D :||

97. **Jane Says** (Jane's Addiction) → ||: G A :|| (two chords in one bar)

98. **Hell N' Back** (Bakar) → ||: G | G | Am | Am :||(capo on 1)

99. **Blurred Lines** (Robin Thicke) → G D (each chord is four bars long)

100. **Three Is A Magic Number** (Blind Melon) → ||: D G :||

101. **Lively Up Yourself** (Bob Marley) → ||: D | G :||

102. **What I Got** (Sublime) → ||: D G :||

103. **Stop Whispering** (Radiohead) → ||: D | G :||

104. **Anyone Else But You** (Moldy Peaches) → ||: G | G | C | C :||

105. **Look So Fine, Feel So Low** (Paul Kelly) → ||: C | G :||

106. **Molly's Lips** (Nirvana) → ||: G C :|| (two chords in one bar)

107. **One World** (Not Three) (The Police) → ||: G | F :||

108. **Silence Is Easy** (Starsailor) → ||: E | E | A | A :||

109. **Oye Como Va** (Santana) → ||: Am | D :||

110. **505** (Arctic Monkeys) → ||: Dm | Dm | Em | Em :||

111. **Dance the Night Away** (The Mavericks) → ||: D | A :||(capo on 2)

112. **Born in the USA** (Bruce Springsteen)

 ||: A | A | A | A | D | D | D | D :||(capo on 2)

DAY SIX

DAY 6

More Two-Chord Songs

In the following two-chord songs, the chord changes are no longer repeating in the more evenly spaced, repetitive way as in the previous songs. These following songs are a bit more challenging. You can't look at your hands as much anymore here for these songs, as you will want to read the chords while playing along with the song, so you know when to change chords. Play as many of these songs as you like to. The more you play, the better you'll get.

113. **Tennessee Whiskey** (Chris Stapleton)

    ||: G | Am | Am | G :|| (capo on 2)

    This song is actually in 12/8, which we didn't cover a strum rhythm for.

    You can still play it, though. For now: strum this following rhythm along with the beat:

    down up down – up down up - down up down – up down up

    Hit on every arm motion → 12 hits = 1 bar.

114. **Give Peace a Chance** (John Lennon) → (capo on 1)

    Verse: C

    Chorus: ||: G | G | G | G | C | C | C | C :||

The song form:

Verse + Chorus + Verse + Chorus + Verse + Chorus (repeat & fade)

115. **Paperback Writer** (The Beatles)

Intro: C G (1 hit each, on "back" and on "ter") + G | G | G | G

Verse ||: G | G | G | G |

| G | G | G | G |

| C | C | G | G :||

+ Intro + Verse + Intro

Ending: G (repeat & fade)

116. **Never Can Tell** (Chuck Berry)

(skip the intro)

Verse

||: C | C | C | C |

| C | C | G | G |

| G | G | G | G |

| G | G | C | C :||

117. **Free Falling** (Tom Petty)

||: D Dsus4 | Dsus4 D A :||

Hit every notated chord once, downstrokes only.

118. **When Loves Comes to Town** (BB King, U2)

Intro E | E | E | E

Verse: E | E | E | E |

| E | E | E | E |

Chorus: | A | A | E | E |

| E | E | E | E

Song form:

Intro + Verse + Chorus + Chorus +

Verse (solo) + Chorus + Solo = Verse (10 bars)

+ Verse + Chorus +

Ending Solo = E (14 bars) + ||: A | A | E | E :|| (repeat & fade)

119. **Achy Breaky Heart** (Billy Ray Cyrus)

Intro: A | A | A | A |

Verse: ||: A | A | A | E | E | E | E | A :||

120. **Eleanor Rigby** (The Beatles)

Chorus: ||: C | C | Em | Em :||

Verse: ||: Em | Em | Em | C | C Em ||

Interlude: ||: Em | Em | C | Em :||

Verse

Interlude

Chorus

Verse

Interlude

121. **Break On Through** (The Doors)

Intro ||: Em D :|| 6x

Verse: ||: Em D :||4x

D | D |

Chorus: Em | Em | Em | Em | Em | Em

Intro ||: Em D :|| 4x

Verse + Chorus

Keyboard solo: ||: Em D :||

Verse + Chorus

Bridge: | Em | Em | Em | Em | D | D |

Chorus

122. **Jambalaya** (Hank Williams)

Intro: G| G | C | C |

Verse: ||: C | C | G | G | G | G | C | C :||

123. **Lady in Black** (Uriah Heep)

Intro: Am | Am |

Verse: ||: Am | Am | G | Am :||

Chorus: Am | G Am | Am G | Am ||

Verse + Chorus + Verse + Chorus + Verse (longer) + Chorus (repeat + fade)

124. **Tom Dooley** (The Kingston Trio) → (capo on 2)

Intro: D | D | A | A | A | A | D |

D | D | D | A | A | A | A | D |

Verse: ||: D | D | D | A |

A | A | A | D :|| 9x

Ending: A | D | A | D | A | D ||

125. **Tulsa Time** (Eric Clapton)

Intro: G | G | G | G |

G | G | G | G |

Verse: ||: G | G | G | D | D | D | D | G :|| 3x

Instrumental: : G | G | G | D | D | D | D | G || G

Verse 4x

Instrumental: ||: G | G | G | D | D | D | D | G :|| (repeat & fade)

126. **Tonight's the Night** (Neil Young)

Chorus: ||: D | C :|| 8x

Verse: ||: D | D | D | D :|| 4x

Chorus 4x

Verse

Chorus 4x

Instrumental = verse (16 bars of D)

Verse (10 bars)

Chorus (repeat D | C)

127. **Singin' in the Rain** (Gene Kelly)

Starting the vocal melody

||: F | F | F | F |

F | F | C | C |

C | C | C | C |

C | C | F | F :||

Keep repeating this chord progression till 1:44, where the song modulates to another key for the rest of the song.

128. **Dream Baby** (Roy Orbison)

Intro: F | F |

Verse: C | C | C | C |

C | C | C | C |

F | F | F | F |

C | C | F | F |

(keep repeating the verse)

129. **Reuben's Train** (The Dillards)

(start strumming when the guitar starts at 11 seconds, after the three guitar bass notes).

Intro: F | F | F | F | F

Verse: ||: F | F | F C | F :|| 2x

Instrumental: ||: F | F | F C | F :|| F | 2/4 F |

Verse

Instrumental (minus the 2/4 bar)

Verse

Instrumental (the 2/4 is now a 4/4 bar)

Verse

130. **Iko Iko** (Dixie Cups)

Verse ||: F | F | F | C | C | C | C | F :||

F | F | F | F

(keep repeating this whole chord progression)

131. **The Name Game** (Sherry Ellis)

The musical form and structure are the most challenging part of this song, with varying verse lengths and the occasional added C bars. On the bright side, that makes this song a good chord sight-reading and listening exercise.

Intro: C | C | C | C |

Chorus: ||: C | C | F | C | C | C :||

Verse: ||: C | C | C | C | F | F | C | C :|| 3x

F | F | C | C | C | C |

Chorus: C | C | F | C | C | C |

Bridge: F | F | C | C |

Verse 2: C | C | C | C | F | F | C | C |"

C | C |

(Musical break/talking/no playing)

(1:54) C | C |

Chorus: ||: C | C | F | C | C | C :|| 4x

C | C

Instrumental Outro

||: C | C | C | C | F | F | C | C :||

132. **Just My Imagination** (The Temptations)

Intro: C | C | C | C

Verse: ||: C | F :||

After the musical break (strum again when bass comes in):

| C | C | C | C | C | C | G / G | (G at 2:50)

C | C | C | C | C | C ||

Verse: ||: C | F :|| (repeat & fade)

133. **Love Is a Stranger** (Eurythmics)

Intro = ||: C | C | C | C :||

Verse ||: C | C | C | C | F | F | F | F :||

Chorus ||: F | F | F | F | C | C :|| C | C :||

Verse

Bridge: 8 bars F + 2 bars C

Chorus

Bridge

Chorus (repeat and fade)

134. **Chewing Gum** (Annie)

Intro: C | C F | F | F C |

Verse: C (8 bars)

Pre-Chorus: C | C F | F | F C | C | C F | F | F |

Chorus: ||: C | C F | F | F C :|| C | C ||

Verse + Pre-Chorus + Chorus (4x, minus last 2 C bars)

Bridge: C | C | C | C | C F | F | F C |

Chorus

135. **The Bum Song** (Harry McClintock) (capo on 1st fret)

Intro: C | C | C |

Verse ||: C | C G | G | G C :|| (repeat x times)

Add an extra C bar after the fourth, sixth, and tenth verse repetition.

DAY 6: More Two-Chord Songs | 73

136. **Sodeo** (Raffi)

   Intro: C (8 bars)

   Chorus: ||: C | C | C | G C :|| 4x

   Verse: C (28 bars)

   Chorus: ||: C | C | C | G C :|| 2x

   Verse (fades out)

137. **Rockin' Pneumonia & Boogie Woogie Flu** (Huey Smith)

   ||: C | C | C | C |

   G | G | C | C :||

138. **Fever** (Peggy Lee)

   Intro = ||: Am | Am | E | Am :||

   Verse = ||: Am | Am | Am | Am | Am | Am | E | Am :|| (5x)

   Then that all moves up one fret. (You could potentially quickly put a capo on the first fret and keep playing). Then it moves up a fret again.

   1x intro 2 + 2x 2nd verse (capo on 1)

   1x intro 3 + 4x 3rd verse (capo on 2)

   Ending: E | Am (4x)

DAY SEVEN

DAY 7

Notable Easy Three-Chord Songs

Naturally, I understand that you probably won't have had the time to play all the songs under yesterday's list. That would actually have been pretty crazy if you had somehow managed to find the time to play them all — it's a lot of music. While today, you could choose to play some more of the above two-chord songs you haven't had a chance to discover yet, I would suggest you try out some of the following three-chord songs instead.

Without a doubt, switching between three chords in songs is a next-level challenge. The good news is that you have made such great progress to this point, you are now at a level where you can totally pull these off.

All the next songs are just extra icing on the cake. You've already succeeded in what you set out to accomplish with this book: you can pretty much play one hundred songs on guitar, and it only took you about a week. So here's the next level. There is no particular order for those next songs. You can play these in any order you choose.

139. **Dreams** (Fleetwood Mac)

    The whole song is ‖: F | G :‖

Except for the 8-bar instrumental bridge that starts on the second "You Know" lyric.

The chords in the bridge are:

| F | G | G | F |

| Am | G | G | F |

140. **Thank U** (Alanis Morissette) → ||: C | C | G | F :||

141. **Knockin' on Heaven's Door** (Eric Clapton version of this Bob Dylan song)

    ||: G | D | Am | Am :||

142. **Sweet Home Alabama** (Lynyrd Skynyrd) → ||: D C | G :||

143. **What's Up** (4 Non Blondes)

    ||: G | G | Am | Am | C | C | G | G :|| (capo on 2)

144. **Wicked Game** (Chris Isaak) → ||: Am | G | D | D :| (capo on 2)

At this point, if you can play the above songs, there isn't much holding you back anymore from being able to strum any song you want.

Songs with More than Three Chords

145. **Fly Away** (Lenny Kravitz) → ||: A C | G D :||

146. **Hey Joe** (Jimi Hendrix) → ||: C G | D A | E | E :||

And there you have it! Mission accomplished!

Even if you took two or three weeks to reach this point, you still learned a hell of a lot and gained a vast amount of skills, in a very short amount of time. Congratulations are in order!

I didn't want to leave it at that. I always like to give a bit extra. The following extra chapters touch on some theory, teach you how to play any song you want using transposition, cover some more cool chords, and show you how to play a really important strum rhythm that you will use all the time.

How to Play Flat and Sharp Chords

All the chords you've learned so far give you access to many tens of thousands of songs you can now play. But you might already have come across chord charts to songs you wanted to learn, with chords that consist of a chord name that included a little "b" or "#" placed behind the letter, as in the chord names Bb and Dbm, or C# and F#m.

The lowercase letter b is the music symbol we use for "flat." The # symbol means "sharp." A chord becomes flat when you move it one fret toward the headstock. When you do so, you moved to a chord that sounds lower in pitch. A chord becomes sharp when you move it one fret toward the guitar body, making it sound higher in pitch.

However, you can't do this with the chords you learned so far. All the chords we've covered contain some open string notes that are part of the chord. For example: for an E chord, we only press down three strings with our fingers, but we hit all six strings. Right? The strings we hit that don't have fingers on them are called "open strings." All the chords you've learned so far are physically relatively easy to play because we only need two or three fingers to play each of them. While we strum all six strings, there are only two or three strings to finger notes on. The rest of the notes in each of those chords are played by the open strings (which relieves us from having to use additional fingers to play those notes).

But while that makes those chords physically easy to play, the presence of those open strings in the makeup of the chord also means that, unless you use a capo, you cannot simply move the fingered part of those chord shapes you learned up and down the neck to play b and # chords. You'd only move the part of the chord that is formed by your fingers, but not the rest of the chord that consists of open strings. Let's say as an example, that you see a G# chord in a song. Using the logic that G# is what you get when you move G up a fret toward the guitar body, you'd think you could just move the G chord, you know, one fret up. For fun, try it out so you see what I mean. Finger a G chord, and move the big triangle shape that your fingers form one fret up, then hit all six strings. It sounds pretty dissonant, right? Or play a C shape and move your three fingers up a fret, or up three frets, and strum that.

As you can tell, simply moving the chord up one fret doesn't sound like the sharp chord. A G# chord is supposed to sound like a G chord, just a bit higher in pitch. Instead, the sound you get when you hit that G chord shape moved one fret up is pretty horrible. It sounds completely different in nature. G sounds lovely, open, peaceful, and happy. G# is supposed to have those same sonic qualities, just higher than G. But what you get when you strum that G shape moved up a fret is completely different. It sounds dissonant, harsh, angry, ugly, and dark. That is also the case when you move any of the other chord shapes you learned up or down a couple of frets and then hit all six strings. Playing any of those chords on different locations on the neck creates those dissonant sounds, because you're basically hitting two chords simultaneously: the fingered portion or shape of the chord, which by nature of moving it up or down, became another chord, and the part of the chord in its original position, that you're hitting but that you *didn't* move — the open strings. In other words, when you move a G shape one fret up, those three fingered notes now sound like a G# chord, but the three open strings, which form a G chord, still are played as open strings, resulting in a G# chord (the three fingered notes) and a G chord (the three open strings) sounding simultaneously. Hitting two different chords simultaneously sounds a bit like two people talking over one another in two different languages: Painful, dissonant, clash-y!

The only way you could make this work is if you were to also move the open strings along with the shape formed by the fingers. You can probably already picture, though, how physically challenging that is on the hand muscles. You literally have to free up your index finger, requiring you to play all shapes with your middle finger, ring finger and pinky, so you can use your index finger as a capo that you place behind the moved chord shape. Does that make sense? The following picture might help understanding. The diagram shows how not only the three fingered notes are moved up a fret, but the open strings as well. This chord is a G# chord, because all six notes of the original G chord have simultaneously moved up one fret to the notes of a G# chord. When you try this following chord out, though, you'll realize that this is literally quite a stretch.

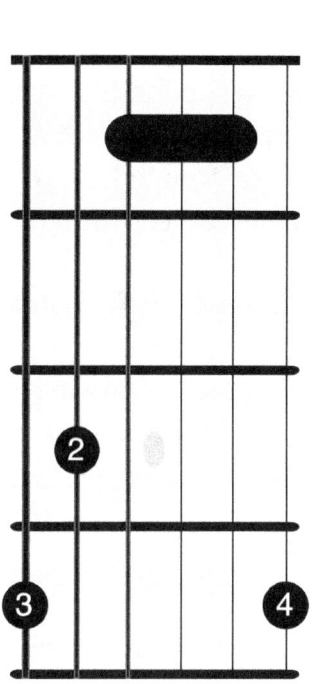

G#

We have a name for this technique where you move a chord shape up or down the neck while using your index finger as a capo. We call these chord fingerings "bar chords." Most of the chord shapes you've learned so far, are simply not practical to be moved around as bar chords. You see what I mean when you try this G# chord fingering: it takes too much work and effort to play that shape. That is why guitar students learn different fingerings for a G# chord, that are unrelated to the G chord shape and that are much easier to play than this chord fingering, which (due to its physical challenge) is impractical for use in most songs or musical situations.

You've likely only been playing for about a week or maybe a couple of weeks the most at this point. It is way too early to get into bar chords — even for the easier bar chord fingerings, they are physically quite demanding on the hand muscles for beginner guitar students. Most guitar students only get to bar chords after about four or five months of playing.

However: wouldn't it be great if, in the meantime, there was some sort of trick or system that would make it possible for you to also already play those songs as well *(or at least some of them)* that have Bb, and F#, and G#, and Eb, and Ab major and minor chords? As turns out, there are a couple of ways to circumvent the problem of not yet using bar chords.

Transpose the Music

You actually, without knowing it at the time, already did this for some of the songs you learned. Anytime you use a capo to play a song in a different key than the original key, you are transposing that song. We used this approach to be able to play the song "Papa Was A Rolling Stone," which is in the key of Bbm. You don't know how to play a Bbm chord, but you didn't let that stop you from playing this song. We transposed a shape we did already know, Am, up a fret to Bbm by moving it up with a capo on the first fret, so we could play this Bbm song. You can keep moving your capo up to each of the twelve frets we have on a guitar. Doing so makes it possible to play one song, in all twelve keys.

Let's say you want to play a song that consists of the C, F, and G chords, in the key up a half step. Put a capo on the first fret and play those C, F, and G chord shapes you already know. Those chords now sound like C#, F#, and G# because you moved the shapes up a fret with a capo. Move it up one fret again, now placing your capo on the second fret, your C, F, and G chord shapes now sound like D, G, and A. As you keep moving up a fret at a time, you keep walking up the alphabet. Up two frets from there, on the fourth fret, your C, F, and G now sound like E, A and B. You see a C chord shape formed by your fingers, but it sounds like E; you see an F shape, but it sounds like A; you see a G shape, but it sounds like a B chord, because you transposed your three chord shapes up four frets with a capo to another higher key. That is why many singer-songwriters use capos. They might write a song, but then find out that they have a hard time singing it. They might find that the song is lower than what they are vocally capable of, or too high, where they have to strain to be able to sing the upper notes. There is an easy fix for that. They just move the chords to the song they wrote up or down the neck with a capo, to a key that falls comfortably within their vocal range. That is called transposition.

Transposition is what musicians do when they play a song in a key other than the original key of the song. I know quite a lot of self-taught piano players who do it all the time. It is a common habit among lesser trained pianists to learn or play every song in the key of C instead of the song's original key, because the C major scale is the easiest of all the scales to learn. It is especially easy to see and learn on piano because it is made up of the white keys of the piano. The notes in that scale are: C D E F G A B. No sharps or flats (black keys) in that scale. Think of how much easier it is to learn any song if you play any song that exists with the same seven notes over and again, instead of with its original notes. There are only seven notes to worry about instead of twelve, and those notes are the same for *all* songs, if you play all songs in that key. There are of course always exceptions to everything. Though the majority of songs only use the seven notes of a scale, there are songs that use more than those seven notes. Going into the reasons why songs in the key of C can also have added # and b notes and chords is beyond the scope of this book. In any case, the same reasoning still holds: those songs are still a lot easier to play in the key of C than they would in their original key. On the downside, pianists who play a lot in the key of C miss out on the cool colors of the other eleven major scale keys. Their playing lacks a lot of color and can get monotonous after a while.

All that said, using a similar approach, you can use Amazing Slow Downer to tune songs up or down to keys for which you already know most or all of the chords.

Let's say that you want to learn a song, and you find out that it is in the key of Bb (which you can tell because it starts on a Bb chord). The following graph shows what the chords are in a Bb scale, and which chords you get when you tune a song in the key of Bb up two half steps to the key of C.

Key	I	IIm	IIIm	IV	V	VIm	VIIdim
Original	Bb	Cm	Dm	Eb	F	Gm	Adim
Transposed to	C	Dm	Em	F	G	Am	Bdim

When you ignore the diminished chords, which aren't used all that much in pop and rock songs, you see that for a song in the key of Bb, you only know two chords, Dm and F. However: when you tune that song up two frets (which we call a "whole step" in music theory), to the key of C, you can now play the whole song cause you already know all the chords in the key. You would just have to make sure to hit a C chord when you see Bb in the chord chart, and a Dm chord when the chord chart tells you to play Cm, and so on. That is easily done by simply quickly rewriting the chord chart you find on the internet, in which you replace every chord of the top row with the chord in the same column from the row right underneath it.

Just like the piano players I talked about, you could technically play *every* song in the key of C. The following table shows the transpositions.

Key	I	IIm	IIIm	IV	V	VIm	VIIdim
Transposed to	C	Dm	Em	F	G	Am	Bdim
Original keys	Db	Ebm	Fm	Gb	Ab	Bbm	Cdim
	D	Em	F#m	G	A	Bm	C#dim
	Eb	Fm	Gm	Ab	Bb	Cm	Ddim
	E	F#m	G#m	A	B	C#m	D#dim
	F	Gm	Am	Bb	C	Dm	Edim
	F#	G#m	A#m	B	C#	D#m	E#dim

Transposed to							
	Gb	Abm	Bbm	Cb	Db	Ebm	Fdim
	G	Am	Bm	C	D	Em	F#dim
	Ab	Bbm	Cm	Db	Eb	Fm	Gdim
	A	Bm	C#m	D	E	F#m	G#dim
	Bb	Cm	Dm	Eb	F	Gm	Adim
	B	C#m	D#m	E	F#	G#m	A#dim
Transposed to	C	Dm	Em	F	G	Am	Bdim

The vertical column labeled with the Roman Numeral "I" shows, from top to bottom, all the twelve notes that exist in music, walking up starting from C, to the next key of the piano (or fret on a guitar), Db, to D, to Eb, over and over again till we hit C again twelve notes later. Notice how from C in the top row to B at the bottom row, I actually listed thirteen notes. That is because I listed both names for the note that falls between F and G, which can be called F# and also Gb. Black keys of the piano, or in other words, notes that are called # or b, have two names: a b name and a # name.

- C# and Db, are two different names for the note that falls between C and D.
- D# and Eb, are two different names for the note that falls between D and E.
- F# and Gb, are two different names for the note that falls between F and G.
- G# and Ab, are two different names for the note that falls between G and A.
- A# and Bb, are two different names for the note that falls between A and B.

In music theory, different names for the same sound are called "enharmonics." C# and Db are enharmonic note names: different names for the same note. The reason for me listing both the keys of F# and Gb in the above table is that both F# and Gb are equally commonly used scales. For reasons that have to do with music theory and that fall beyond the scope of this book, the same is not true for other enharmonic keys. The key of Bb is a very common key, while nobody would write songs in the key of A# (which is why that is not listed in the above table). You will find songs in the key of Ab, but not in the key of G#, which is why G# is not listed in the table.

How to Use the Table Above

Each column in the table above shows you for each chord in any key what you would have to replace that chord with if you wanted to play that song in the key of C. For example: the chord listed for any key in the column that is labeled IIIm needs to be replaced with an Em chord if you transpose to the key of C. The chord listed in the column V for any key needs to be transposed to a G chord (or in other words: replaced with a G chord) when played in the key of C.

Take this following chord progression in the key of Eb.

Eb | Fm | Ab | Bb ||

When you compare the chords in the above chord progression to the columns in the table, you see that this chord progression corresponds to the scale numbers (also called scale degrees) I IIm IV V (in the key of Eb, or in other words, in the Eb row).

Looking at how the chords and those numbers in the key of Eb relate to the chords in the key of C, you get the following:

Key	I	IIm	IIIm	IV	V	VIm	VIIdim
Transposed to	C	Dm	Em	F	G	Am	Bdim
Original keys	Eb	Fm	Gm	Ab	Bb	Cm	Ddim

The table shows that the scale degrees I IIm IV V in the key of C give you the chord progression:

C | Dm | F | G ||

Hence, this chord progression in the key of Eb → Eb | Fm | Ab | Bb |, becomes the following chord progression in the key of C:

C | Dm | F | G ||

You basically replace the chord of the original key with the chord in the same column (scale degree) in the row that show the chords in C (which is the first and the last row in the table).

That way, you can now literally play any song, regardless of what key it's in. Not knowing all the chords in all keys is no longer a hindrance. You simply transpose any song to a key you already know all the chords for.

What If You Want to Play Along with the Song?

It's always good to play along with a song you're learning, as you then also improve your timing, rhythm playing, ensemble playing, listening skills, and so much more. To that end, you'd need to transpose the song file up or down to the key of C, using Amazing Slow Downer. After all: you couldn't play the chords of the C scale while the song is sounding like it's in another key. The chords of the song's original key would clash with the chords you are playing. Both you and the song file need to be in the same key. As luck would have it, the table also shows how far up or down you'd need to transpose any song in any key for it to sound like it's in the key of C.

Each row in that table represents a half step. Each row is a half step up in pitch from the row above it. Conversely, each row is also a half step down in pitch from the row underneath it. To illustrate this: the key of Db (second row) sounds a half step higher than the key of C (first row), and the key of C sounds a half step lower than the key of Db. The key of B sounds a half step lower in pitch than the key of C, and the key of C sounds a half step higher than the key of B. The half step is the smallest interval we have in music: it's the distance between two adjacent keys on a piano, which corresponds to two adjacent frets on a guitar. You might also see the term "semitone" being used, which is another music theory name for half step.

Using the above table as an example:

Key	I	IIm	IIIm	IV	V	VIm	VIIdim
Transposed to	C	Dm	Em	F	G	Am	Bdim
Tune this key	Db	Transpose songs in this key (Db) down a semitone					

Transposed to							
D	Transpose songs in this key down two semitones						
Eb	Transpose songs in this key down three semitones						
E	Transpose songs in this key down four semitones						
F	Transpose songs in this key down five semitones						
F#	Transpose songs in this key up or down six semitones						
Gb	Transpose songs in this key up or down six semitones						
G	Transpose songs in this key up five semitones						
Ab	Transpose songs in this key up four semitones						
A	Transpose songs in this key up three semitones						
Bb	Transpose songs in this key up two semitones						
B	Transpose songs in this key up a semitone						
C	Dm	Em	F	G	Am	Bdim	

How about Songs in Minor Keys?

While there are always exceptions, you can usually tell what key a song is in by looking at the first chord of a song. When a song starts on a Fm chord, that song is almost always in the key of F minor.

To start off with some great news: you don't have to learn everything completely from scratch again for minor keys. Turns out that for each major key/scale in the above table, there is a minor key/scale that consists of all the same chords. In music theory, this is called "relative scales." Relative scales are different scales that consist of the same seven notes, and hence share the same seven chords. The minor key that is relative to C major, for example, is A minor. To reiterate what that means, it means that the A minor scale, and the C major scale consist of the same notes and chords.

C major scale: C D E F G A B

A minor scale: A B C D E F G

While both these scales consist of the same seven notes, they are very different scales with very different sonic identities. The C major scale sounds happy, the A minor scale sounds sad.

The best way to hear that, is by hitting:

- A C chord first, and then play or sing the notes of the C scale, C D E F G A B
- An Am chord first, and then play or sing the notes of the Am scale, A B C D E F G

What makes a song be in the key of C versus in the key of Am is the chord the song starts on and the fact that, in good songwriting, the song keeps regularly coming back to that chord. It's that starting chord, and the fact songs keep coming back to it throughout the song, that gives songs their major scale (happy song) or minor scale (sad song) sonic quality.

The following table shows how to transpose songs in all twelve minor keys to the key of A minor.

Key	I	IIdim	bIII	IV	V	bVIm	bVII
Transposed to	Am	Bdim	C	Dm	Em	F	G
Original keys	Bbm	Cdim	Db	Ebm	Fm	Gb	Ab
	Bm	C#dim	D	Em	F#m	G	A
	Cm	Ddim	Eb	Fm	Gm	Ab	Bb
	C#m	D#dim	E	F#m	G#m	A	B
	Dm	Edim	F	Gm	Am	Bb	C
	D#m	E#dim	F#	G#m	A#m	B	C#
	Ebm	Fdim	Gb	Abm	Bbm	Cb	Db
	Em	F#dim	G	Am	Bm	C	D

	Fm	Gdim	Ab	Bbm	Cm	Db	Eb
	F#m	G#dim	A	Bm	C#m	D	E
	Gm	Adim	Bb	Cm	Dm	Eb	F
	G#m	A#dim	B	C#m	D#m	E	F#
Transposed to	**Am**	**Bdim**	**C**	**Dm**	**Em**	**F**	**G**

Compare the above table that lists all the minor keys to the table listing all the chord in all major keys. Notice how C major and A minor indeed share the same seven chords, and the same for all the other scales/rows down the list in both tables.

Now you can also play all songs written in any minor key. You simply transpose the song's chords to the chords in the key of A minor, the same way as was explained earlier for major keys. If you want to play along with the actual song recording, you would use Amazing Slow Downer to transpose the song file up or down the number of rows (semitones) that each key is removed from the key of A minor. For example, a song in the key of C minor needs to be transposed down three semitones for it to be in the key of A minor (Cm is three rows up from Am). Remember that with each row toward the floor, or in other words down the page, the pitch goes up a half step. A song in the key of G minor needs to be transposed up two semitones to sound like it's in the key of A minor, because G minor sounds a whole step (two half steps) lower in pitch from the Am at the bottom of the table. Notice how Gm is down (in pitch, musicians always think in sound, not physical location) two rows from Am. Don't let the fact that it visually looks two rows higher on the page fool you. Remember that the list sonically moves from low notes at the top of the table to high notes at the bottom.

An important point I want to conclude with is that I am not advocating you only play music in two keys, the key of C and the key of A minor. That would go against everything I stand for as an educator. It would be a shame to miss out on discovering all the cool other colors that come with each key. Each key has its own unique distinct tonal color. The key of A, for example sounds very vibrant, outgoing, open, and inviting, while the key of Eb sounds very soft, softspoken, warm, fuzzy like a soft blanket, and intimate. That is why pianists who choose to play every song in the key of C only, because they then only have to deal with white keys, miss out on a lot of the musical colors and musical richness that each key provides.

The only reason for me teaching the above info about transposition, is that this gives you tens of thousands more songs that you can play besides the ones listed in the book. More precisely: you are now pretty much able play almost any and every pop and rock song ever written, just not necessarily in their original keys (for now). All of this gives you a vast amount of extra, fun material you can use to further practice your already acquired skills, which also buys you time to strengthen your dexterity, hand strength, and rhythm skills. This further prepares you and gives you tons of material to have fun with, in attendance of the time when your hands will be strong enough to learn bar chords, which will be in no time.

If you diligently practice songs (playing along with the song) with the chords you already know, for say, about an hour a day, it might only take five to six weeks for you to gain the hand strength necessary to learn Bb, Bbm, B, Bm, C# (and the enharmonic Db), C#m (and the enharmonic Dbm), Eb, Ebm, F#, F#m, G#, and G#m chords, all of which are played as bar chords.

Once you've learned those chords, you no longer have to transpose songs to the key of C or A minor. You then know all the chords in every major and minor key. You can then play almost any song you want, in its original key. Very exciting! I'm saying "almost," because you might come across the occasional song which might have a diminished or other chord you have not yet learned.

Branching Out from There: Bar Chords

Looking back at the two tables listing the chords in all major keys and minor keys, and again, ignoring the less frequently used diminished chords, notice how you:

- Know all the chords in the key of C and the key of A minor.

- Are only one chord short of knowing all the chords in the keys of G and E minor (the chord Bm).

- Are only two chords short of knowing all the chords in the keys of D and B minor (the chords F#m and Bm).

- Are only two chords short of knowing all the chords in the keys of F and D minor (the chords Gm and Bb).

Building further on those facts, it stands to reason that you'd get the most progress if you learn the Bm chord next. Learn just that one chord and you can play all songs in the keys of G and E minor (again, ignoring the VIIdim chord, which is rarely used in pop or rock songs).

Bm

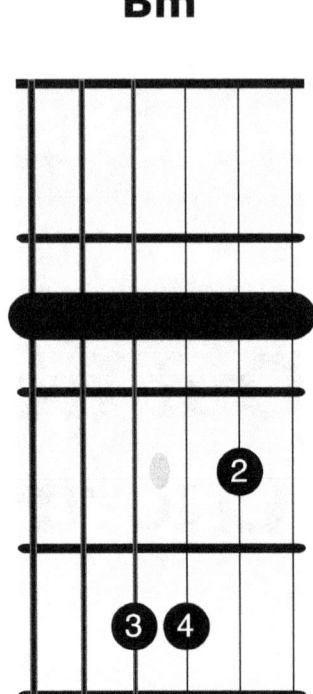

Now that you also know all the chords in the key of G, you start to have options. New possibilities open up. The above table, which shows how to transpose chords in any key to the key of C, can also be used to figure out how to transpose to other keys than the key of C. Let's say you want to learn a song that is in the key of A, but you want to play it in the key of G (because you now know all the chords in that key). It's just a matter of counting how many rows the keys are removed from one another in the table in relationship to one another. If you already know all the chords in the key of G, you can simply transpose the song in the key of A down a whole step (two semitones/rows) to the key of G, instead of transposing it up three semitones to the key of C. To reiterate how to do this: you simply replace A chords with G chords (the I column in the A and G rows), and Bm chords with Am chords (the IIm column in the A and G rows), and so on. If you want to play along with the actual song, you can then either:

1) Transpose the actual song file that is in the key of A, down two semitones with Amazing Slow Downer. The tuned-down song then sounds like it's in the key of G. In this scenario, you tune a song that is in a key that you don't know all the chords for yet (the key of A) down to a key that you do know how to play, the key of G.

2) Keep the song file in its original key but place a capo up two semitones, meaning on the second fret, and play the chords of the key of G, which will now sound like they're in the key of A. You are essentially playing chords of a key that is a whole step down (two semitones down) from the original key (A), the

key of G, up a whole step with a capo. When you play the chords of a G scale up a whole step (two semitones), they sound like the chords of an A scale.

I hope this makes sense. It takes a while to get used to these concepts. You might have to read the above a couple of times for it to click. You can also just skip or ignore it and simply use whatever system makes the most sense to you. Either way, over time, you will find that all this will start to make sense automatically as your musical knowledge keeps growing.

In any case, it's a ton of fun when you can start playing music in different keys.

The same above approach applies to minor keys. Example: A song you want to learn turns out to be in the key of Dm, but you don't know all the chords yet in that key. You do, however, know the chords in the key of E minor — they are the same chords as in the key of G. G major and E minor are relative scales. Rather than having to retune/transpose the Dm song to the key of Am, which is a big distance, you can just transpose it up two semitones to the key of E minor instead. You then replace the chord in the I column in the Dm row with the chord in the I column of the Em row, and the chord in the IIdim column in the Dm row with the chord in the IIdim column of the Em row, and so on.

Some Bar Chord Logic

Coming back to the above Bm chord diagram: notice how it looks like an Am chord shape, moved up two frets with the index finger barring on the second fret. That is exactly what bar chords are. They are chords in which you use your index finger as a capo, which moves the nut of the guitar forward along with the chord shape. Also notice the logic: as you move up toward the guitar body, away from the nut, chord names move up alphabetically. If you were to move the above Bm chord, up one fret to the third fret, the name of that chord is Cm, up another fret to the fourth fret is C#m, up another fret, Dm, etc. You, again, can use the table above to figure out the chord names of bar chords. The table shows that Bm comes two rows after Am. Conclusion: moving an Am shape up two frets makes a Bm chord. Three rows up from Bm in the table shows Dm, hence moving a Bm chord up three frets (from the second to the fifth fret), is where you play a Dm chord.

Use that same logic to learn the next best bar chord to learn.

The next chord you should learn is F#m. That is the only piece of information you need to learn next to be able to play songs in the keys of D and Bm. Guess how the above logic applies to an F#m chord? You can probably deduce it from the following chord diagram.

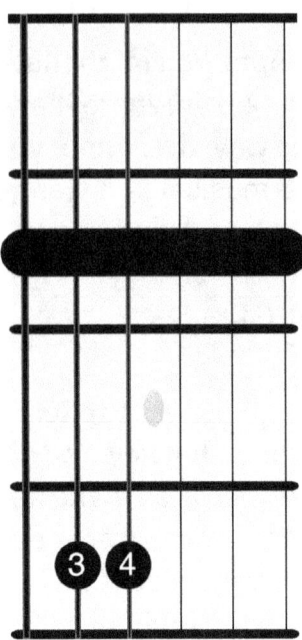

F#m

Yes: we play F#m as an Em chord shape moved up the alphabet to F#m. You can see on the table with minor keys that Em and F#m are two rows apart. This translates on the guitar to those two chords being two frets apart. F#m in the table comes two rows after Em. Building further on that logic, on a guitar, F#m is two frets up (toward the guitar body) from Em, which, as you know, is played with open strings. Open strings are sounded by the guitar nut, which is also sometimes called the "zero fret." Moving up two frets from zero → 0 + 2 = 2. Meaning: F#m, which is two frets above Em, is going to be on the second fret, since Em is on the zero fret (a.k.a. open strings).

I'm not trying to confuse you by overexplaining it a bit. I am trying to give you different explanations and directions, all leading to the same conclusion. Usually, students understand things more deeply or more quickly when they are presented with different explanations coming from different angles and viewpoints, all explaining the same thing.

Also notice how the first two bar chords you learned, Bm and F#m, are both on the same fret. One is an Am shape moved from the zero to the second fret, and the other is an Em shape moved from the zero to the second fret.

Meanwhile: making your first steps into learning your first bar chords, one at a time, gets your hand and finger strength to keep evolving to the next levels very gradually. Now that you know all the chords in a D scale, you can transpose songs in the key of Db up a half step to the key of D, or songs in the key of Eb down a half step to D. You can transpose songs in the key of E down a whole step to the key of D, or songs in the key of F down three semitones to the key of D. The number of rows that each key is removed from the key of D in the table shows how many semitones you'd have to transpose songs up or down to sound like they're in the key of D.

I, IV, V

While you have those tables showing all seven chords in the major and minor scales in all twelve keys, most songs actually only use a couple of those chords. There are so many songs that only use three or so chords. Here's some quick composition and songwriting knowledge: a vast majority of songs are written only using the first, fourth, and fifth chord in a scale. This has to do with how those chords "feel," or one could say "function," within a scale.

As you probably know, songs are sonic stories. Songwriting is storytelling. All good storytelling, whether it is in movie making, novel writing, visual arts, or music, follows certain reoccurring principles that are integral to the telling. Every story starts with a beginning, where things feel relaxed and where you get introduced to the main character. That is exactly what the first chord in a scale feels like: a home base, a starting point. No surprise there, considering that the first chord of a scale is the starting point of the scale. Then that main character somehow gets restless or curious or somehow gets prompted to embark upon an adventure of some sort. That is what chord number IV in a scale feels and acts like. It feels like we're going somewhere. We're not home anymore. The IV chord brings a certain excitement: we're out and about, where do we go from here? During that protagonist's trip or adventure, suddenly there is a certain danger, or obstacle, or huge problem or challenge that tests that main character's intelligence, skills, courage, inventiveness or resourcefulness. You, the spectator to the story, get deeply engaged in the story here. You're wondering: How is that protagonist going to get out of this? You're anxious to find out what is going to happen next. It's a tense situation: you feel for the protagonist, you feel the tension, you can't wait to find out how this situation is going to get resolved. That is exactly what the V chord in a scale (the fifth chord in the major scale) feels like. It brings tension to the song. That is why, in music theory, we call V in a major scale the dominant. That chord dominates the chord progression. It is the chord that contains the most tension of all the chords in a scale, and it wants to resolve back to I. As such, the V chord creates strong forward momentum in a song — its need to resolve to I creates momentum and direction to the flow of a song.

How does all that help you with learning new songs as a beginner? Well, since a majority of songs are written only using I, IV, and V in any given key, that means that you could add a huge number of mastered songs to your repertoire by only learning how to play the first, fourth and fifth chord in any scale.

The table shows that in the key of E, those chords are E, A, and B. We haven't covered the B chord yet. Luckily, there is an open-string fingering version for B that you could use in this case.

Here it is:

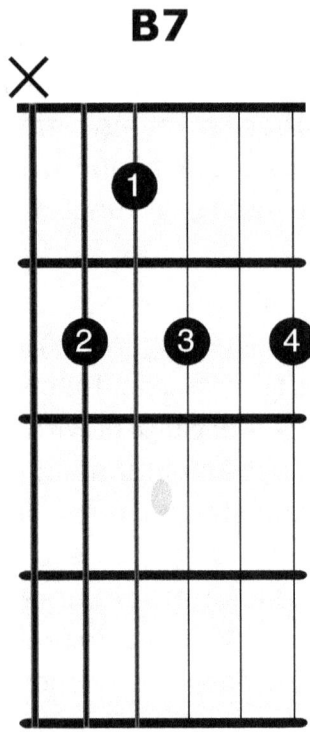

Here's I IV V in all twelve major keys.

Key	I	IV	V
C major scale	**C**	F	G
Db major scale	**Db**	Gb	Ab
D major scale	**D**	G	A
Eb major scale	**Eb**	Ab	Bb
E major scale	**E**	A	B
F major scale	**F**	Bb	C
F# major scale	**F#**	B	C#
Gb major scale	**Gb**	Cb	Db
G major scale	**G**	C	D
Ab major scale	**Ab**	Db	Eb
A major scale	**A**	D	E
Bb major scale	**Bb**	Eb	F
B major scale	**B**	E	F#

For minor keys, it's the same chords as above, but played as minor chords.

In other words:

- I IV V in major scales are major chords.
- I IV V in minor scales are minor chords. (Im, IVm and Vm)

Blues Songs

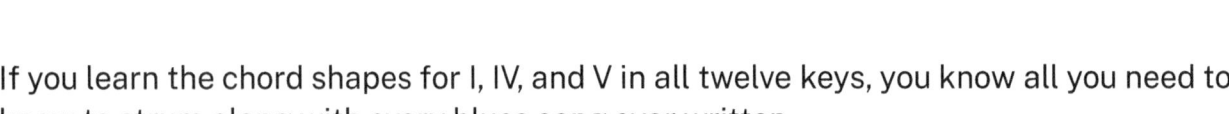

If you learn the chord shapes for I, IV, and V in all twelve keys, you know all you need to know to strum along with every blues song ever written.

One of the things that makes blues blues is its form and structure. Blues songs don't have choruses, pre-choruses, verses and bridges. Blues songs consists of one song section that keeps on repeating over and again. Not only that: that song section is also very much set in stone.

1) It's always twelve bars long.

2) There are only three chords: I, IV, and V.

3) Those three chords are played at exactly the same locations in every blues song. It's called the "twelve-bar blues form."

When you memorize that twelve-bar form, you can pretty much strum along the majority of all blues songs. Here's all twelve bars, and where the chords need to be played over those bars:

||: I | IV | I | I |
IV | IV | I | I |
V | IV | I | V :||

The Roman numerals show which chords to play; the horizontal lines you see between the Roman numerals are called "bar lines." They show that there are twelve bars, and that every bar has one chord. In minor blues, the form is exactly the same, but those chords are simply all played as minor chords.

||: and :|| are called repeat signs, as discussed earlier. Musicians use these music notation symbols to communicate that the music that is written between those two symbols needs to be repeated.

When you translate the above scale degrees to chord names in, for example, the key of A, the chord progression is:

||: A | D | A | A |
D | D | A | A |
E | D | A | E :||

In an A minor blues, it's the same chords in exactly the same order, but all minor (Am, Dm and Em) instead of major.

The most common variations on the above blues form are:

||: I | I | I | I |
IV | IV | I | I |
V | IV | I | V :||

Notice that the only difference is that this blues form stays on the I chord in the second bar, instead of going to the IV chord.

Another variation is:

||: I | I or IV | I | I |
IV | IV | I | I |
V | IV | I | I :||

In this variation, the song section ends on the I chord instead of on the V chord, creating a bit more of a static feel.

There are more possible variations on the above forms, but they're far less common than the above progressions. The above three forms sum up the majority of blues songs.

A final word: when you strum along with blues songs, you will not necessarily sound like a blues guitarist. The reason for this is that blues guitarists don't usually strum chords, but play specific rhythm and note patterns that are part of what makes the language of blues. All that said, you can play along with the blues songs by just strumming chords, using the songs for your timing, chord, and strumming practice.

If you want to really learn how to play some mean blues guitar, you are definitely ready at this point to tackle that goal. Having reached this point in the book means that you have acquired the skills necessary to explore blues guitar (or any other music styles you might be into). You simply need to contact me at vreny@zotzinmusic.com or 310-902-0993 to set up your blues lessons (or whatever else you would like to get much better at on guitar, in a very short amount of time).

The Most Commonly Used Strum Rhythm

Anyhow . . . there you have it. When you've reached this point in the book, you now know or can play thousands of songs. Mission accomplished! You're practically ready to front your own cover band as a rhythm guitarist. ☺ After all, you know enough songs to play three- to four-hour shows.

I want to give you one little extra thing before closing. This is the most commonly, most heavily used strum rhythm. Sometimes it seems like most guitar players play this rhythm 99 percent of the time.

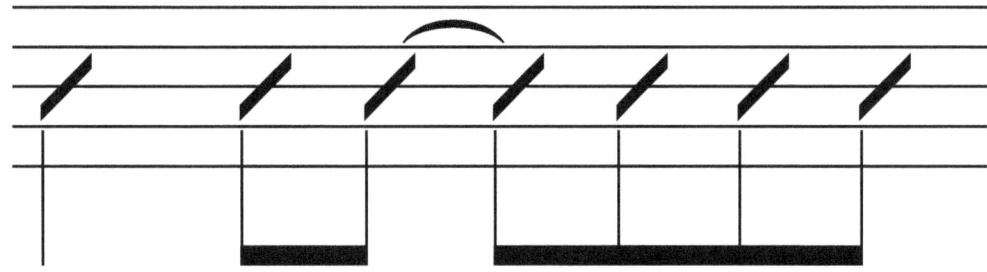

Here's how to play this rhythm:

First beat: hit *miss*

Second beat: hit hit

So far so good, right? That is the rhythm you've been playing in past seven days.

We're halfway through this new rhythm, and so far it's exactly the same as the one you can already play. Moving on:

Notice the curved line between the third and the fourth slash in the above music notation? This symbol is called a tie. That tie connects the rhythmic duration of the slash at the end of beat 2 to the rhythmic duration of the slash on beat 3, turning these combined rhythmic durations into one longer duration. In other words: we don't hit the note/chord on beat 3 because it is tied to the sound we hit on beat 2.

Third beat: *miss* hit (miss the strings in the down motion, and hit the strings in the up motion).

How did that feel? That might need practice. So far, you haven't played a rhythm yet where we missed the strings on the down motion. Most people in the beginning struggle with the coordination it takes to move the strum arm down without hitting the strings.

Fourth beat: hit hit (That one's easy, right?)

Putting this all together, we get: down *miss*   down up   *miss* up   down up

Some quick pointers that might speed up your ability to learn or play this rhythm:

1) The whole rhythm consists of eight arm motions total (four times "down up").

2) This rhythm pattern consists of one hit, then two hits, then three hits, all separated with a space (miss). ONE miss, ONE TWO miss, ONE TWO THREE. (Hit once, miss, hit twice, miss, hit three times). You'd hit again on the next arm motion after that, because that is where the whole rhythm pattern starts over again. Students often find it easier to perform or learn the rhythm after they realize that they can just count groupings of one, then two, and then three hits, separated by an in-between miss.

3) It feels unnatural, in the beginning, to not hit on a down-motion. That is what happens on the second miss in the rhythm. One trick that helps overcome the coordination challenge you might encounter there is to "push" your hand down right on that miss, with a lot of force. Exaggerating the downward motion in size and force on that miss (the fifth arm motion), tends to help students get a sense of how it feels like to miss on a down motion, and prevents them from getting stuck (choking) there in that part of the rhythm.

You might need another week before this rhythm clicks or feels natural. Have fun with it. You can use it in most of the songs we covered.

In Closing

Congrats on making it this far.

How did you do? Did you enjoy this crazy ride? Did you think you could learn this much or that many songs so well in such a short time? I wish I could hear you play right now and see how far you've come in only one week.

This, of course, is just the beginning.

If you thought *that* was fun, you're in for many fun surprises on your guitar journey, because it keeps getting exponentially more fun and more rewarding the better you keep getting at guitar.

There's really nothing quite like the amazing feeling you get when you impress friends and loved ones with your performance of an impressive song or guitar solo that you had to practice hard to master. That feeling can't be put into words — it's something one needs to experience to truly fathom the depths of joy and satisfaction.

If you want to reach that level way faster than you'd think possible, check out https://www.zotzinguitarlessons.com and contact me to start lessons.

In the meantime...

Keep rocking!

FOR EVEN FASTER PROGRESS,
SIGN UP FOR THE VIDEO LESSON PACKAGE
THAT TEACHES EVERYTHING IN THIS BOOK AT:

GuitarVoyage.com/BeginnerGuitarBootcamp

This video package is custom designed for you: the owner of this book. The videos:

- Teach you how to tune.

- Explain how capos work and how to use the practice tools.

- Teach proper technique, hand position, and posture for optimal guitar playing, as well as contain regular repetition and reminders to make sure you keep up great technique and practice habits till they become second nature.

- Show you how to play all the chords.

- Teach you how to play each rhythm covered in the book.

- Contain practice sessions. These are play-along sessions where you have me as your personal trainer guiding you to your best possible performance as fast as possible. My students LOVE these training videos, so much that they often prefer playing along with them rather than with the actual songs.

- Give your learning structure and organization. Simply following the videos in order will get you through this book in no time and will get you to indeed be able to play over 100 songs in a week or less, if you so desire.

- Are short, fun, productive, and focused.

- Offer extra free lessons that are not covered in this book, and that will keep you improving and learning for many more months to come, way past what this book offers.

Acknowledgements

A Special Word of Thanks To:

Dylan Garity for the amazing work he did getting my manuscript in shape, improving my language, wording, and so much more. I'm so happy to have you on my team.

Ani Boyadjian, my very dear friend and the principal librarian at Los Angeles Public Library, who helped me with the copyright page and guided me in improving this book. I can't begin to tell you how honored I feel that you contributed the copyright page in my book. Now we're even more connected for life, and I love that.

Lazar Kackarovski for the fantastic job done on the inner page design and book design. I don't know what I would have done without your amazing expertise.

My amazing best friends David Crocco and Cela Scott: You know how much I love you.

All my many music, guitar, songwriting, and composition teachers, who all shared their knowledge, skills, and insights with me. I am forever grateful.

My hundreds of colleague musicians I've performed, jammed, or recorded with in the past thirty-plus years. I can only imagine the many more fun music adventures that await us.

My students, who are making all this possible, and who keep propelling me forward to constantly improve things. I obviously could never have done any of this without you.

The over one thousand authors and researchers whose books I've read in the past thirty years on psychology, pedagogy, music education, neuroscience, NLP, and learning styles.

Mum and Dad and my sister and her family: Thank you for always being there for me. I'm sure I sometimes must have driven you nuts with my loud guitar solos and the many hours of practicing every day.

Last but not least, the love of my life and extraordinary wife: Tiannah York Van Elslande. I'm so lucky and blessed I get to share my life with you. We'll keep laughing our butts off together for eternity, sweetie. And of course, the other love of my life: Aiden, my lovely son, I love you. The last song about you has not been written yet.

About The Author

Vreny Van Elslande is considered one of SoCal's top guitar and music teachers. His client roster includes numerous famous musicians, actors, celebrities, and entertainment people.

Born in Ypres, Belgium in 1971, Vreny started playing guitar when he was sixteen. He completed a ten-year classical guitar & composition study in seven years with high honors. He then moved to Boston to study at Berklee College of Music, where he graduated Summa Cum Laude with two degrees, in Guitar Performance and Music Production & Engineering.

In 2002, Vreny left Boston for Los Angeles, where he restarted his teaching business. He performed and co-wrote songs with various artists, won songwriting awards, appeared on TV in the US and Belgium, got his songs on the radio, and reached twelfth place on the Billboard charts. Vreny LOVES vanilla and ube ice cream, Suhr guitars, The Beatles, Queen & ABBA, long walks and hikes, teaching, writing, playing guitar, reading, writing music, playing with his son, and rocking out. He happily lives in Santa Clarita with his wife Tiannah and son Aiden.

Review

Before you go, I wanted to say thank you for purchasing this book. You could have picked from hundreds of other guitar books, but you took a chance and chose this one.

So thank you for choosing it and studying it all the way to the end.

If you enjoyed this book and feel that you learned a lot, please help me spread the word by posting a review on Amazon. You'd be supporting an independent artist and helping other people find the value you found in this book. I'd be very grateful if you'd post a short review.

Your support really does make a difference. I read all reviews personally, so I can get your feedback and make this book even better. This feedback also helps me continue to write the books that will help you get the results you want.

So if you enjoyed it, please let me know.

Thank you very much. It means a lot to me!

Contact Info

Website: https://www.ZOTZinGuitarLessons.com

Phone: 310-902-0993

Email: info@zotzinmusic.com

Facebook: https://www.facebook.com/ZOTZinMusic
Twitter: https://twitter.com/ZOTZinMusic
Yelp: https://www.yelp.com/biz/vrenys-guitar-lessons-los-angeles
YouTube: https://www.youtube.com/user/ZOTZin